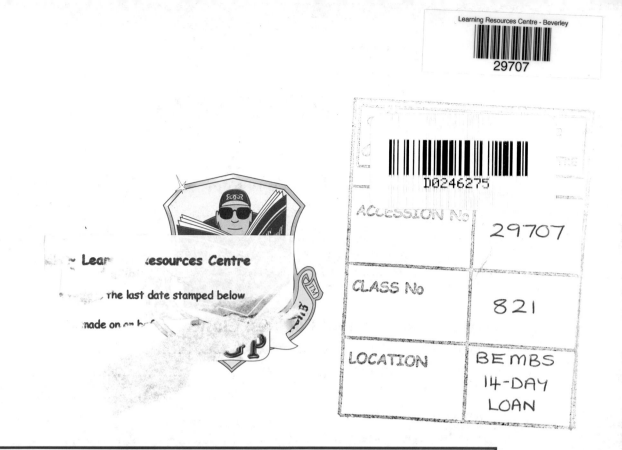

~ Lear ...esources Centre

... the last date stamped below

...made on ...

GCSE English AQA Anthology

The Study Guide

Poems from Different Cultures

AQA A Specification — Foundation Level

This book is a step-by-step guide to becoming an expert on the Anthology part of your GCSE English exam.

It's got everything you need to know — annotated poems, exam themes and worked essays.

It's ideal for use as a classroom study book or a revision guide.

CONTENTS

Section Two — The Themes

Section Three — How to Answer the Question

Published by Coordination Group Publications Ltd.

Contributors:
Charley Darbishire, Roland Haynes, Kate Houghton,
Kate Redmond, Katherine Reed and Edward Robinson

With thanks to Sue Hirst, Elisabeth Sanderson and Kate Houghton for the proofreading.

ISBN: 1-84146-698-0

Groovy website: www.cgpbooks.co.uk

Jolly bits of clipart from CorelDRAW

Printed by Elanders Hindson, Newcastle upon Tyne.

How To Use This Book

This book will help you do better in your **GCSE English Anthology Exam**. It's full of straightforward ways of getting **extra marks**. Start by asking your teacher which poems and themes you need to study: some schools get you to study all of them, others pick out certain ones.

There are Three Sections in this book

Section One is all about the Poems

There are **two pages** about **each poem**. This is what the pages look like:

The **poem** is on the left hand page, along with other useful features:

- There's a nice picture of **the poet** and some info about their life.

- Important or tricky bits of the poem are **highlighted** and **explained**.

- Difficult words are explained in the **poem dictionary** at the bottom.

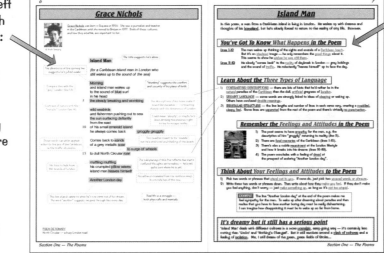

On the right hand page there are **notes** about the poem. They talk about:

- **What happens** in the poem.

- The **language** the poet uses.

- The **feelings** of the poet.

- A bit that will help you to decide what **you think** of the poem.

Read through the pages on the poems you've been told to study. When you've read about each poem, shut the book and write out as much as you can remember. See what you left out, then do it again. It's boring, but a **great way to learn**.

Section Two is about the Themes

In the exam, you'll have to **compare** how **two poems** relate to one of the **themes**. There's a page about each of the main themes that might come up in your exam. The pages tell you which poems use each theme and how different poets treat the same theme. **Read it**, **understand it** and **learn it**.

Section Three is About Preparing for Your Exam

Section Three is about the **CGP Five-Step Method**™ which helps you to write essays that get **good marks**.

The pages on the left explain the CGP **Five-Step Method** of answering exam questions.

This method helps you **use the information** you learn in Sections One and Two to write good essays.

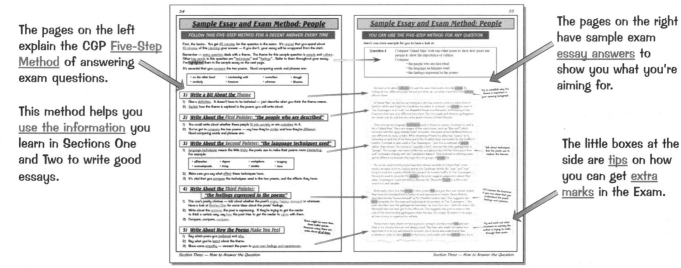

The pages on the right have sample exam **essay answers** to show you what you're aiming for.

The little boxes at the side are **tips** on how you can get **extra marks** in the Exam.

Write some **essays** using the **Five-Step Method**. Use the exam-style questions in the CGP Anthology Workbook, if you have it, or ask your teacher for some practice questions. You get **45 minutes** to answer the 'Poetry from Different Cultures' question in the Exam, so practise doing some **timed essays**.

Edward Kamau Brathwaite

knees spread wide
and the water is hiding

> This suggests the low ceilings of the decks of the ship, and also leaning back for the limbo dance.

30 *limbo*
limbo like me

> Repetition emphasises the bad conditions on the ship.

knees spread wide
and the dark ground is under me

35 down
down
down

> He almost dies on the ship.

and the drummer is calling me

> The drum offers hope — it's like a friend to him.

limbo
limbo like me

> This line is the turning point of the poem — darkness is replaced by light.

40 sun coming up
and the drummers are praising me

out of the dark
and the dumb gods are raising me

> New hope — he's lifted out of the darkness.

45 up
up
up

> He survives the voyage.

and the music is saving me

> The slow three step beat shows he's tired but still alive.

hot
50 slow
step

> The full stop at the end — the only one in the poem — represents the end of the dance, of the voyage, and perhaps his life.

on the burning ground.

> This fiery image could suggest he's reached hell.

POEM DICTIONARY
Limbo has several meanings —
1. The West Indian dance, crouching backwards to pass under a horizontal stick — said to have originated from the memories of travelling in the cramped decks of the slave ships
2. An imaginary place for unwanted or forgotten people
3. In Christianity, a place where infants who die before baptism go

Section One — The Poems

Edward Kamau Brathwaite

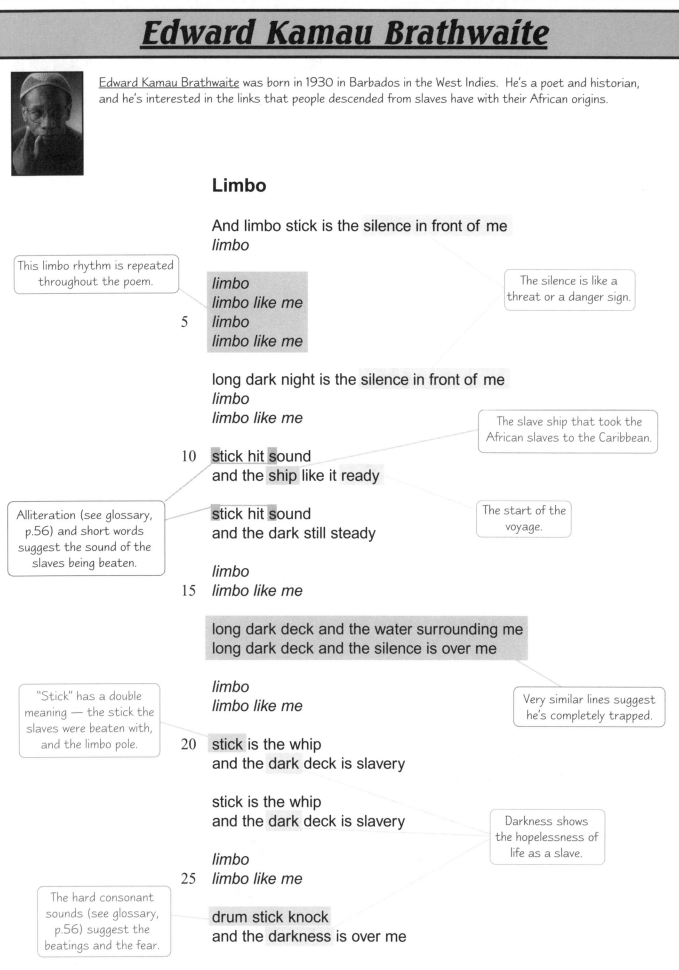

Edward Kamau Brathwaite was born in 1930 in Barbados in the West Indies. He's a poet and historian, and he's interested in the links that people descended from slaves have with their African origins.

Limbo

And limbo stick is the silence in front of me
limbo

> The silence is like a threat or a danger sign.

> *limbo*
> *limbo like me*
> 5 *limbo*
> *limbo like me*

> This limbo rhythm is repeated throughout the poem.

long dark night is the silence in front of me
limbo
limbo like me

10 stick hit sound
and the ship like it ready

> The slave ship that took the African slaves to the Caribbean.

stick hit sound
and the dark still steady

> The start of the voyage.

> Alliteration (see glossary, p.56) and short words suggest the sound of the slaves being beaten.

limbo
15 *limbo like me*

long dark deck and the water surrounding me
long dark deck and the silence is over me

limbo
limbo like me

> Very similar lines suggest he's completely trapped.

> "Stick" has a double meaning — the stick the slaves were beaten with, and the limbo pole.

20 stick is the whip
and the dark deck is slavery

stick is the whip
and the dark deck is slavery

> Darkness shows the hopelessness of life as a slave.

limbo
25 *limbo like me*

> The hard consonant sounds (see glossary, p.56) suggest the beatings and the fear.

drum stick knock
and the darkness is over me

THIS IS A FLAP.
FOLD THIS PAGE OUT.

Limbo

This poem uses the <u>limbo dance</u> to describe the cruel journey taken by African people on <u>slave ships</u> to the Caribbean colonies. So understandably, it's not a barrel of laughs.

You've Got To Know What Happens in the Poem

<u>Lines 1-19</u>   Two main themes are introduced — the <u>limbo dance</u>, and the voyage of a <u>slave ship</u>.

<u>Lines 20-36</u>   The middle of the poem is the <u>middle of the voyage</u>, right under the stick or limbo pole.

<u>Lines 37-51</u>   In the final section, the poet sees an <u>end to the suffering</u>. He comes "out of the dark" at last — although where he ends up might be worse than the journey.

Learn About the Four Types of Language

1) <u>REFERENCES TO SLAVERY</u> — this is the main theme. We see the <u>cruel conditions</u> that the slaves had to put up with.

2) <u>REPETITION</u> — the lines "*limbo / limbo like me*" are repeated throughout the poem. Some lines are repeated with <u>minor differences</u>, e.g. lines 16 and 17.

3) <u>METAPHORICAL LANGUAGE</u> — descriptions of <u>darkness</u> and the <u>slave ship</u> are used to stress the living hell of slavery. The voyage of the ship is used as a metaphor for the <u>suffering</u> of the slaves.

4) <u>RHYTHM</u> — the beat of the <u>drum</u> on the ship is like the <u>dull repetition</u> of slave labour. Also, the tribal beat of the <u>limbo dance</u> recalls the slaves' African roots.

Remember the Feelings and Attitudes in the Poem

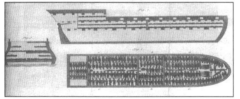

Plan of a slave ship

1) He's <u>angry</u> at the <u>conditions</u> on the cramped slave ship and the <u>cruelty</u> the slaves have suffered (e.g. line 20).

2) But he <u>admires</u> the strength of the slaves.

3) He <u>celebrates</u> the slaves' past — and their <u>survival</u> (line 47).

> We experience a mixture of emotions in 'Limbo' — we feel the slaves' <u>fear and suffering</u> but also their <u>joy in survival</u>.

Think About Your Feelings and Attitudes to the Poem

1) Pick two words or phrases that <u>stand out to you</u>. If none do, just pick two <u>unusual words or phrases</u>.

2) Write these two words or phrases down. Then write about how they <u>make you feel</u>. If they don't make you feel anything, don't worry — just <u>make something up</u>, as long as it's <u>not too stupid</u>.

> **EXAMPLE** On line 41, the poet says "The drummers are praising me". Up to this point, the dance has stood for the cruelty of slave life, but it seems to me that the music is now a positive thing — I think the drummers are his African ancestors, helping him out of the hell of slavery.

Talk about the effect of the poem as a whole

The poem is <u>one long sentence</u>. This helps to create the feel of a <u>continuous dance</u>, and the never-ending suffering of the slaves. Having "And" as the first word suggests this isn't the start of the suffering — it's been going on for <u>generations</u>.

Tatamkhulu Afrika

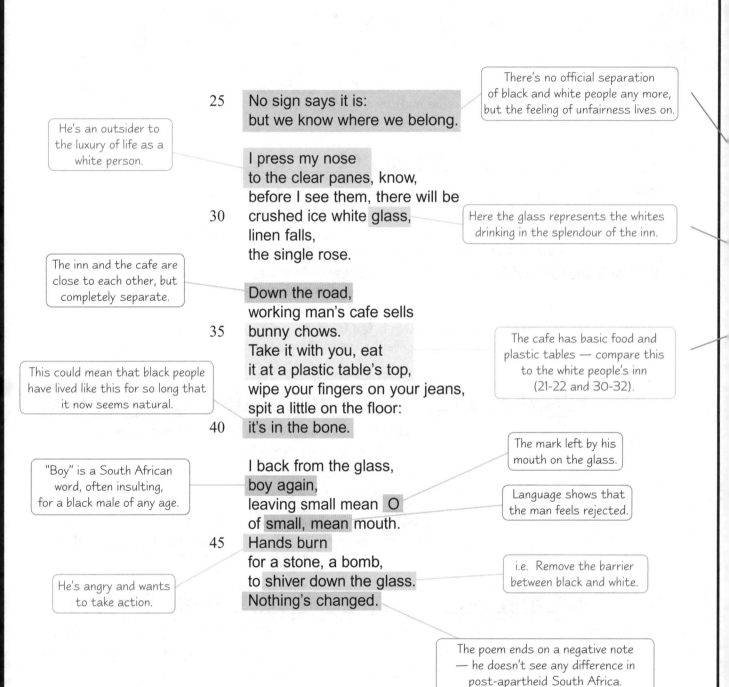

There's no official separation of black and white people any more, but the feeling of unfairness lives on.

He's an outsider to the luxury of life as a white person.

25 No sign says it is:
but we know where we belong.

I press my nose
to the clear panes, know,
before I see them, there will be
30 crushed ice white glass,
linen falls,
the single rose.

Here the glass represents the whites drinking in the splendour of the inn.

The inn and the cafe are close to each other, but completely separate.

Down the road,
working man's cafe sells
35 bunny chows.
Take it with you, eat
it at a plastic table's top,
wipe your fingers on your jeans,
spit a little on the floor:
40 it's in the bone.

The cafe has basic food and plastic tables — compare this to the white people's inn (21-22 and 30-32).

This could mean that black people have lived like this for so long that it now seems natural.

I back from the glass,
boy again,
leaving small mean O
of small, mean mouth.
45 Hands burn
for a stone, a bomb,
to shiver down the glass.
Nothing's changed.

The mark left by his mouth on the glass.

"Boy" is a South African word, often insulting, for a black male of any age.

Language shows that the man feels rejected.

i.e. Remove the barrier between black and white.

He's angry and wants to take action.

The poem ends on a negative note — he doesn't see any difference in post-apartheid South Africa.

POEM DICTIONARY
amiable — likeable / friendly
incipient — developing, just starting
Port Jackson trees — large pine trees
haute cuisine — high-class, expensive food
bunny chows — cheap food for the poor

Tatamkhulu Afrika

Tatamkhulu Afrika (1920-2002) was born in Egypt but raised as a white South African.
When apartheid was introduced, he refused to be classed as a "superior" white.
He joined the African National Congress (ANC) and was a political prisoner because
of his fight against apartheid.

Apartheid was a system of government used in South Africa, where black and "coloured" people were treated as inferior to white people.

Nothing's Changed

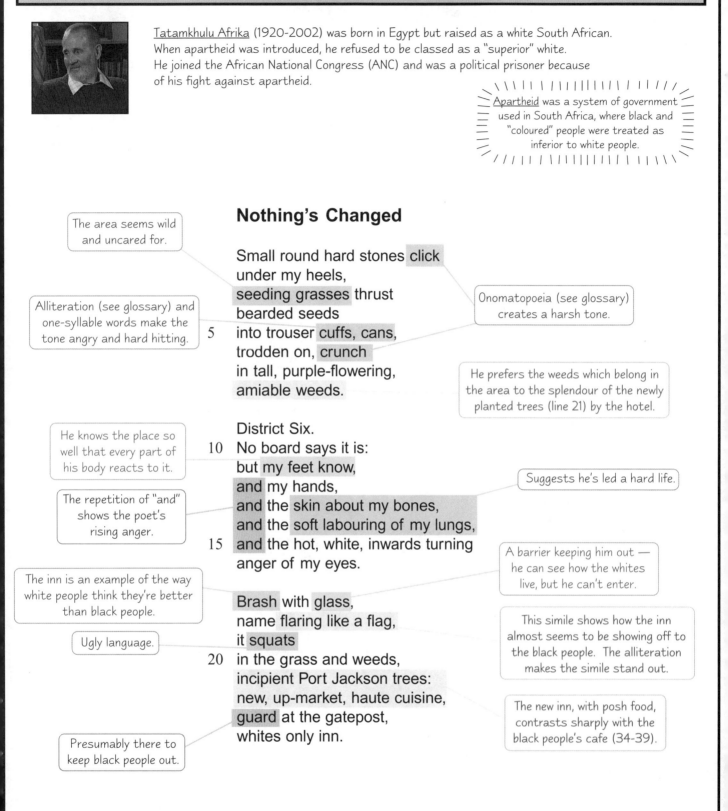

The area seems wild and uncared for.

Alliteration (see glossary) and one-syllable words make the tone angry and hard hitting.

Onomatopoeia (see glossary) creates a harsh tone.

He prefers the weeds which belong in the area to the splendour of the newly planted trees (line 21) by the hotel.

> Small round hard stones click
> under my heels,
> seeding grasses thrust
> bearded seeds
> 5 into trouser cuffs, cans,
> trodden on, crunch
> in tall, purple-flowering,
> amiable weeds.
>
> District Six.
> 10 No board says it is:
> but my feet know,
> and my hands,
> and the skin about my bones,
> and the soft labouring of my lungs,
> 15 and the hot, white, inwards turning
> anger of my eyes.
>
> Brash with glass,
> name flaring like a flag,
> it squats
> 20 in the grass and weeds,
> incipient Port Jackson trees:
> new, up-market, haute cuisine,
> guard at the gatepost,
> whites only inn.

He knows the place so well that every part of his body reacts to it.

The repetition of "and" shows the poet's rising anger.

Suggests he's led a hard life.

A barrier keeping him out — he can see how the whites live, but he can't enter.

The inn is an example of the way white people think they're better than black people.

Ugly language.

This simile shows how the inn almost seems to be showing off to the black people. The alliteration makes the simile stand out.

The new inn, with posh food, contrasts sharply with the black people's cafe (34-39).

Presumably there to keep black people out.

THIS IS A FLAP.
FOLD THIS PAGE OUT.

Nothing's Changed

In this poem, the poet goes back to District Six in South Africa. When he lived there it was a mixed-race area, but after <u>apartheid</u> was introduced, it became "<u>whites only</u>". When he returns, apartheid has officially ended and District Six is supposedly mixed again — but Afrika sees little difference.

You've Got To Know What Happens in the Poem

<u>Lines 1-16</u>　　He describes his return to District Six. He says that, even though the old sign is gone, his <u>senses</u> tell him where he is — "my feet know, / and my hands" (lines 11-12).

<u>Lines 17-32</u>　　This section's about the <u>inn</u>. The inn represents the <u>reality</u> — blacks and whites still don't mix. It's clear that the inn is for <u>white people only</u>.

<u>Line 33-48</u>　　He thinks about the <u>cheap cafe</u> "down the road". It's very <u>different</u> from the inn. In the final four lines, he says he wants to <u>destroy the inn</u>.

Learn About the Three Types of Language

1) <u>HARSHNESS</u> and <u>BITTERNESS</u> — he's angry at the inequality, and uses <u>harsh-sounding words</u>. They're often short words, with <u>alliteration</u> and <u>onomatopoeia</u> (see glossary, p.56) adding to the harsh feel.

2) <u>METAPHORICAL LANGUAGE</u> — The inn represents <u>white superiority</u>. The <u>glass</u> of the inn is like the barrier of apartheid, which you can't see but which is still there.

3) <u>COMPARISONS</u> — the differences between the lives of white and black people give you loads to talk about. Keep an eye out for comparisons split between <u>different verses</u>, e.g. the inn and the cafe.

Remember the Feelings and Attitudes in the Poem

Nelson Mandela —
president of South Africa after apartheid

1) There's the physical <u>recognition</u> of the poet's home district (lines 9-16).

2) But this is tinged with <u>anger</u> at its <u>neglected state</u>, and at the <u>racial inequality</u> that still exists (e.g. line 26).

3) There's <u>bitterness</u> and <u>resentment</u> in his contrasting descriptions of the white people's inn (lines 17-32) and the black people's cafe (lines 33-40).

4) This turns to <u>violent feelings</u> at the end of the poem, when he wants to "shiver down the glass" of the whites only inn (lines 45-47).

Think About Your Feelings and Attitudes to the Poem

1) Pick two words or phrases that <u>stand out to you</u>. If none do, just pick two <u>unusual words or phrases</u>.

2) Write these two words or phrases down. Then write about how they <u>make you feel</u>. If they don't make you feel anything, don't worry — just <u>make something up</u>, as long as it's <u>not too stupid</u>.

> **EXAMPLE** When the poet says, "we know where we belong," it makes me feel angry. Apartheid is supposed to be gone, yet the man in the poem is very aware of the inequalities that still exist. He's made to feel inferior to white people.

Show you know about the subject

The poet's opinion about South Africa is pretty clear cut — so you need to go into a bit more <u>detail</u> than just saying "he reckons it's the same as when apartheid was around". And if you can link a few <u>facts</u> about <u>apartheid</u> or <u>Nelson Mandela</u> to the poem, you'll really wow mean old Mr Examiner.

Grace Nichols

Grace Nichols was born in Guyana in 1950. She was a journalist and teacher in the Caribbean until she moved to Britain in 1977. Both of these cultures, and how they interlink, are important to her.

© Sheila Geraghty

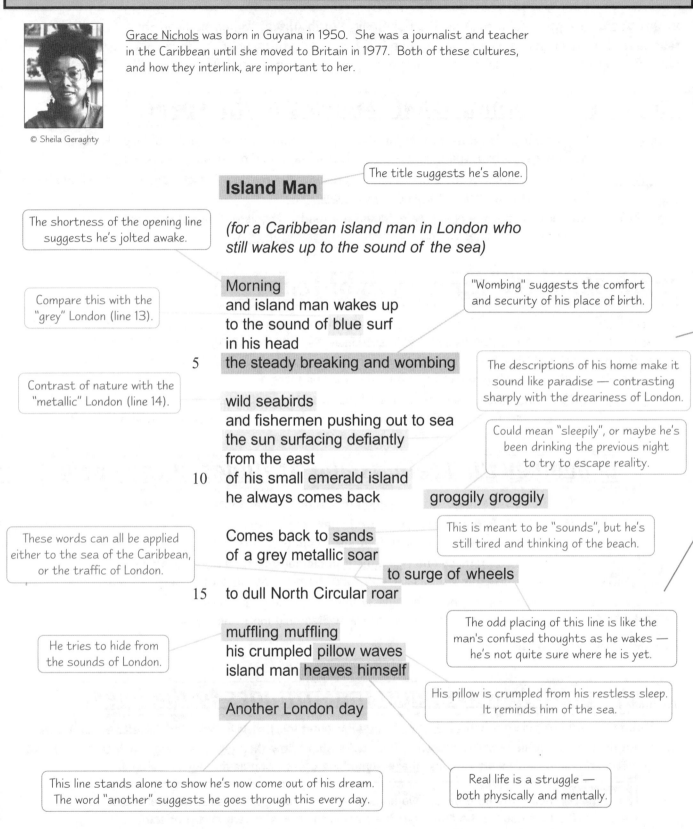

Island Man

> The title suggests he's alone.

(for a Caribbean island man in London who still wakes up to the sound of the sea)

> The shortness of the opening line suggests he's jolted awake.

> Compare this with the "grey" London (line 13).

> Contrast of nature with the "metallic" London (line 14).

> "Wombing" suggests the comfort and security of his place of birth.

> The descriptions of his home make it sound like paradise — contrasting sharply with the dreariness of London.

> Could mean "sleepily", or maybe he's been drinking the previous night to try to escape reality.

> This is meant to be "sounds", but he's still tired and thinking of the beach.

> These words can all be applied either to the sea of the Caribbean, or the traffic of London.

> He tries to hide from the sounds of London.

> The odd placing of this line is like the man's confused thoughts as he wakes — he's not quite sure where he is yet.

> His pillow is crumpled from his restless sleep. It reminds him of the sea.

> This line stands alone to show he's now come out of his dream. The word "another" suggests he goes through this every day.

> Real life is a struggle — both physically and mentally.

```
Morning
and island man wakes up
to the sound of blue surf
in his head
5   the steady breaking and wombing

    wild seabirds
and fishermen pushing out to sea
the sun surfacing defiantly
from the east
10  of his small emerald island
he always comes back          groggily groggily

Comes back to sands
of a grey metallic soar
                    to surge of wheels
15  to dull North Circular roar

muffling muffling
his crumpled pillow waves
island man heaves himself

Another London day
```

POEM DICTIONARY
North Circular — a busy London road

Island Man

In this poem, a man from a Caribbean island is living in London. He wakes up with dreams and thoughts of his homeland, but he's slowly forced to return to the reality of city life. Bummer.

You've Got To Know What Happens in the Poem

Lines 1-10   The man wakes up thinking of the sights and sounds of a Caribbean beach. But it's an idealised image — he only remembers the good things about it. This seems to show he wishes he was still there.

Lines 11-19   He slowly "comes back" to the reality of daybreak in London — grey buildings and the sound of traffic. He reluctantly "heaves himself" up to face the day.

Learn About the Three Types of Language

1) CONTRASTING DESCRIPTIONS — there are lots of hints that he'd rather be in the natural paradise of the Caribbean than the dull, artificial greyness of London.

2) DREAMY LANGUAGE — some words are strongly linked to ideas of sleeping or waking up. Others have confused double meanings.

3) IRREGULAR STRUCTURE — the line lengths and number of lines in each verse vary, creating a muddled, sleepy feel. Some lines are separated from the rest of the poem and there's virtually no punctuation.

Remember the Feelings and Attitudes in the Poem

1) The poet seems to have empathy (see glossary) for the man, e.g. the description of him "groggily" returning to reality (line 11).

2) There are fond memories of the Caribbean (lines 1-10).

3) There's also a resentment of the London lifestyle and how it breaks into his dreams (lines 16-18).

4) The poem concludes with a feeling of dread at the prospect of enduring "Another London day".

Think About Your Feelings and Attitudes to the Poem

1) Pick two words or phrases that stand out to you. If none do, just pick two unusual words or phrases.

2) Write these two words or phrases down. Then write about how they make you feel. If they don't make you feel anything, don't worry — just make something up, as long as it's not too stupid.

> EXAMPLE   The line "Another London day" at the end of the poem makes me feel sympathy for the man. To wake up after dreaming about paradise and then realise that you have to face another boring day must be really disheartening. I can imagine how disappointing it must be to wake up so far from home.

It's dreamy but it still has a serious point

'Island Man' deals with different cultures in a more nostalgic, easy-going way — it's certainly less cutting than 'Limbo' and 'Nothing's Changed'. But it still revolves around a clash of cultures and a feeling of isolation. Me, I still dream of the green, green fields of Stoke...

Imtiaz Dharker

Imtiaz Dharker was born in 1954 in Pakistan. She has said that she believes identity comes from "beliefs and states of mind", rather than nationality or religion.

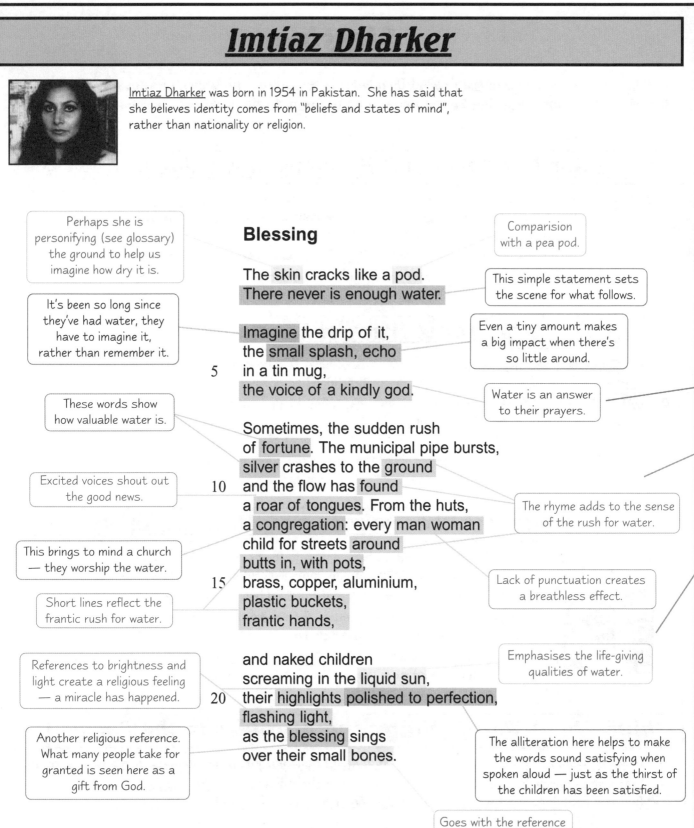

Blessing

Perhaps she is personifying (see glossary) the ground to help us imagine how dry it is.

Comparision with a pea pod.

The skin cracks like a pod.
There never is enough water.

This simple statement sets the scene for what follows.

It's been so long since they've had water, they have to imagine it, rather than remember it.

Imagine the drip of it,
the small splash, echo
5   in a tin mug,
the voice of a kindly god.

Even a tiny amount makes a big impact when there's so little around.

Water is an answer to their prayers.

These words show how valuable water is.

Sometimes, the sudden rush
of fortune. The municipal pipe bursts,
silver crashes to the ground
10   and the flow has found
a roar of tongues. From the huts,
a congregation: every man woman
child for streets around
butts in, with pots,
15   brass, copper, aluminium,
plastic buckets,
frantic hands,

Excited voices shout out the good news.

This brings to mind a church — they worship the water.

Short lines reflect the frantic rush for water.

The rhyme adds to the sense of the rush for water.

Lack of punctuation creates a breathless effect.

References to brightness and light create a religious feeling — a miracle has happened.

Another religious reference. What many people take for granted is seen here as a gift from God.

and naked children
screaming in the liquid sun,
20   their highlights polished to perfection,
flashing light,
as the blessing sings
over their small bones.

Emphasises the life-giving qualities of water.

The alliteration here helps to make the words sound satisfying when spoken aloud — just as the thirst of the children has been satisfied.

Goes with the reference to skin in line 1.

POEM DICTIONARY
municipal — to do with the city

Blessing

Blessing is set in a massive <u>slum</u> called Dharavi, on the outskirts of Mumbai (Bombay). The poem describes the reactions of the people there to a <u>burst water pipe</u>, and how precious water is to them.

You've Got To Know What Happens in the Poem

<u>Lines 1-6</u>   The poet describes the <u>dryness</u> of the slum, caused by <u>drought</u> and <u>no water supply</u>.
                  We get a sense of how every drop of water is <u>precious</u> to the people living in the slum.

<u>Lines 7-17</u>   A water pipe <u>bursts</u> and loads of people frantically gather round to collect as much water
                  as possible with anything that comes to hand (lines 14-16).

<u>Lines 18-23</u>   The <u>children</u> of the slum are described, excited and happy in the water (lines 18-20).

Learn About the Three Types of Language

1)   <u>METAPHORICAL LANGUAGE</u> — the words used to describe water make it seem <u>valuable</u>.
    The people of the slum follow it like a <u>religion</u> (line 12).

2)   <u>CHANGING TONE</u> — each verse has a feel of its own. The dreamy <u>fantasy</u> of water in verse 2 gives way
    to the frenzied pace of the rush when it appears for <u>real</u>. The final verse has a strange, <u>religious</u> feel.

3)   <u>LIFE-RELATED LANGUAGE</u> — the reliance on water for <u>survival</u> is a constant theme.

Remember the Feelings and Attitudes in the Poem

1)   There's a real <u>desperation</u> because of the lack of water — and
       the poet <u>appeals</u> to the reader to imagine how this would feel.

2)   This desperation leads to the frantic <u>urgency</u> in collecting the water.

3)   There's sheer <u>delight</u> at the rare pleasure of having water to drink
       and to play in.

Some water, yesterday

Think About Your Feelings and Attitudes to the Poem

1)   Pick two words or phrases that <u>stand out to you</u>. If none do, just pick two <u>unusual words or phrases</u>.

2)   Write these two words or phrases down. Then write about how they <u>make you feel</u>. If they don't make
    you feel anything, don't worry — just <u>make something up</u>, as long as it's <u>not too stupid</u>.

> **EXAMPLE**   When I read the line "the sudden rush / of fortune", I have mixed feelings.
> I feel happy and relieved for the people who live in the slum, because they have water
> at last, but I also feel sorry for them. Water is something most of us take for granted,
> yet for them it's like a miracle. It makes me feel grateful for what I've got.

This poem's not all it seems

It's an odd poem, this one. It's about people living in <u>poverty</u> and desperate to survive, but the tone seems to be quite upbeat — the people of the slum are <u>ecstatic</u> at the sight of water. But that also highlights just how poor they are. So even though it's short, there's lots to talk about in "Blessing".

Lawrence Ferlinghetti

Lawrence Ferlinghetti was born in New York in 1919. He settled in San Francisco and is interested in how different cultures and races mix. He's concerned about the growing gap between rich and poor people.

Two Scavengers in a Truck,
Two Beautiful People in a Mercedes

The title reflects the poem's contrasts — the disgusting scavengers versus the beautiful rich people.

The whole poem is about this short period of time. It's like a snap-shot.

At the stoplight waiting for the light
      nine a.m. downtown San Francisco
a bright yellow garbage truck
      with two garbagemen in red plastic blazers
5   standing on the back stoop
      one on each side hanging on
and looking down into
      an elegant open Mercedes
with an elegant couple in it
10 The man
    in a hip three-piece linen suit
      with shoulder-length blond hair & sunglasses
The young blond woman so casually coifed
      with a short skirt and colored stockings
15 on the way to his architect's office

And the two scavengers up since four a.m.
      grungy from their route
    on the way home
The older of the two with grey iron hair
20   and hunched back
   looking down like some
      gargoyle Quasimodo
And the younger of the two
    also with sunglasses & long hair
25 about the same age as the Mercedes driver

And both scavengers gazing down
      as from a great distance
   at the cool couple
as if they were watching some odorless TV ad
30   in which everything is always possible

And the very red light for an instant
    holding all four close together
as if anything at all were possible
      between them
35 across that small gulf
    in the high seas
      of this democracy

Annotation boxes:

Repetition adds to the sarcastic tone of this word.

No movement.

Stark contrasts.

They look down at the rich people, but only as carved, stone gargoyles might look down at people in church.

Something in common between the rich and poor.

Another similarity, but only a superficial one.

The gazing is one-way — the rich couple don't pay the binmen any attention.

The couple don't even notice the binmen.

It's just a fantasy, and won't affect or touch them in any way.

It can't actually happen — it's just an illusion.

This moment won't last or change anything.

These two words contradict each other — the gap appears small, but it's impossible to cross.

This reference to democracy is bitter and sarcastic — everyone is supposed to be equal in a democracy.

POEM DICTIONARY
stoop — rear footplate of a truck
coifed — stylishly arranged hair
Quasimodo — the fictional hunchbacked bell ringer of Notre Dame
democracy — government by the people, or whoever they elect

hip — fashionable
gargoyle — a carved monster on the wall of a building
odorless — with no smell (American spelling)

Two Scavengers in a Truck, Two Beautiful People in a Mercedes

This poem describes a frozen <u>moment in time</u> at a San Francisco traffic light. Two pairs of people from <u>different backgrounds</u> "meet". There's some strong <u>social commentary</u> about the gap between the rich and poor. Yeah, right on, fight the system! Anyway...

You've Got To Know What Happens in the Poem

<u>Lines 1-9</u>   Two "garbagemen" (<u>binmen</u> to you and me) look down from their truck to see a rich, attractive couple in a flashy <u>Mercedes</u> car.

<u>Lines 10-25</u>   The stark <u>contrasts</u> between the two pairs of people are described — the <u>trendy clothes</u> and expensive hair-dos of the couple in the Merc, and the <u>dirty</u>, exhausted binmen.

<u>Lines 26-37</u>   The poet describes how <u>far apart</u> the pairs are in social terms, even though they're physically very close. This is dead important to the <u>message</u> of the poem.

Learn About the Three Types of Language

1)   <u>STILLNESS</u> — the poem describes a <u>single moment</u>, and the odd layout spreads the phrases around like the different things you might notice in a <u>photograph</u>. There are <u>no full stops</u> — it's read in <u>one go</u>.

2)   <u>COMPARISONS</u> — there are a few <u>similarities</u> between the rich and poor people, e.g. "sunglasses & long hair" (line 12), but there are also loads of <u>differences</u>.

3)   <u>SOCIAL COMMENTARY</u> — this just means the poet says things about <u>people and society</u>. He often uses <u>sarcasm</u> to show his opinions, e.g. describing the rich people as "Beautiful" and "elegant" (line 8), when he <u>doesn't really admire them</u> at all.

Remember the Feelings and Attitudes in the Poem

My social conscience must be in here somewhere...

1)   The poet is <u>fascinated</u> with the extremes in society.

2)   But he's also <u>critical</u> of society for allowing these extremes, and for making the differences between rich and poor so obvious.

3)   There's a sense of the binmen <u>longing</u> for a life that they <u>can't have</u>.

Think About Your Feelings and Attitudes to the Poem

1)   Pick two words or phrases that <u>stand out to you</u>. If none do, just pick two <u>unusual words or phrases</u>.

2)   Write these two words or phrases down. Then write about how they <u>make you feel</u>. If they don't make you feel anything, don't worry — just <u>make something up</u>, as long as it's <u>not too stupid</u>.

> **EXAMPLE**   When the poet refers to the binmen as "scavengers", it makes me feel disgusted, but also sorry for them — they are forced to live off the scraps of hope offered by seeing how rich people live, and this feels very unfair.

It's set in the good ole US of A — but that's ok...

Ok, so there are words like "downtown", and "coloured" is spelt wrong, which makes it sound a bit yankee-doodle. But the <u>themes</u> and <u>issues</u> in the poem could apply just as much to our lovely old U of K — just substitute San Francisco for Bristol and you get the idea.

Nissim Ezekiel

Nissim Ezekiel was born in Bombay in 1924, to Jewish parents. But he was raised in a mainly Hindu culture, and has been influenced by atheist views (atheists don't believe a God exists).

Night of the Scorpion

It's from the child's point of view.

He uses a straightforward tone to describe the incident.

I remember the night my mother
was stung by a scorpion. Ten hours
of steady rain had driven him
to crawl beneath a sack of rice.

5 Parting with his poison – flash
of diabolic tail in the dark room –
he risked the rain again.
The peasants came like swarms of flies
and buzzed the name of God a hundred times

10 to paralyse the Evil One.
With candles and with lanterns
throwing giant scorpion shadows
on the mud-baked walls
they searched for him: he was not found.

15 They clicked their tongues.
With every movement that the scorpion made
his poison moved in Mother's blood, they said.
May he sit still, they said.
May the sins of your previous birth

20 be burned away tonight, they said.
May your suffering decrease
the misfortunes of your next birth, they said.
May the sum of evil
balanced in this unreal world

25 against the sum of good
become diminished by your pain.
May the poison purify your flesh
of desire, and your spirit of ambition,
they said, and they sat around

30 on the floor with my mother in the centre,
the peace of understanding on each face.
More candles, more lanterns, more neighbours,
more insects, and the endless rain.
My mother twisted through and through,

35 groaning on a mat.
My father, sceptic, rationalist,
trying every curse and blessing,
powder, mixture, herb and hybrid.
He even poured a little paraffin

40 upon the bitten toe and put a match to it.
I watched the flame feeding on my mother.
I watched the holy man perform his rites
to tame the poison with an incantation.
After twenty hours

45 it lost its sting.

My mother only said
Thank God the scorpion picked on me
and spared my children.

These words set the scene by showing it's a poor Indian home.

This simile makes the villagers seem panic-stricken and unwelcome.

The scorpion is seen as symbolic of the devil.

A terrifying image, especially for a child.

They don't seem very bothered about failing to find the scorpion.

The villagers are talking about her reincarnation — they think she'll die.

Sounds like a prayer. But having the same word at the start of so many lines makes this reaction seem repetitive and unthinking. "They said" is also repeated at the end of many lines.

Pain is seen as a way of cleansing the soul before the next life.

There's an ironic feel to this — their reaction has been far from understanding or peaceful.

This shocking sight clearly lives on in the poet's memory, even as an adult.

This shows how desperate the situation is.

All he can do is watch. The holy man's actions seem baffling to him.

The matter-of-fact tone suggests this was expected — the panic was unnecessary.

These words are associated with religious customs and beliefs.

There's a ceremonial feel to the holy man's actions — they don't seem like a practical solution.

POEM DICTIONARY
diabolic — to do with the devil
diminished — reduced
sceptic — a doubtful person
rationalist — a person who uses
logical thinking to explain things
hybrid — a mixture of things
rites — actions in a ceremony
incantation — religious chanting

He admires his mother for staying calm after all she's been through, and through everyone else's panic.

Night of the Scorpion

The poet remembers a time when he was a child when his <u>mother</u> was <u>stung by a scorpion</u>.
He describes the reactions of various <u>religious people</u> — and seems to think they were all a bit silly.
In the end, his mum <u>survived</u> anyway. I love a happy ending...

You've Got To Know What Happens in the Poem

<u>Lines 1-7</u>   The poet remembers how a <u>scorpion</u>, which had come inside to escape the rain, <u>stung his mum</u>.

<u>Lines 8-33</u>   Some locals come round and look for the scorpion, but they <u>can't find</u> the blighter (line 14).
They try to help the woman, saying <u>religious stuff</u> about <u>reincarnation</u> —
they clearly think his mum's going to <u>die</u>.

<u>Lines 34-48</u>   His mum's in <u>agony</u> (lines 34-35). His <u>dad</u> does everything he can to <u>cure</u> her. Then, after
all the fuss, she <u>pulls through</u>, and just thanks God it was her and not her children (lines 47-48).

Learn About the Three Types of Language

1)   <u>FACTUAL TONE</u> — there's a <u>straightforward</u> way of talking when the poet describes
the more action-based parts of the story, e.g. the stinging incident (lines 1-4).
This <u>contrasts</u> with the more ceremonial feel of the <u>religious language</u>.

2)   <u>THE CHILD'S PERSPECTIVE</u> — it's a <u>first person narrative</u>, so we witness the events
through the <u>child's eyes</u>. He's confused and frightened, as any child would be.

3)   <u>RELIGIOUS LANGUAGE</u> — it's set in a Hindu community, where they believe in <u>reincarnation</u>
— so there's lots of stuff about <u>purifying the soul</u> of sin for the <u>next life</u> (lines 19-28).

Remember the Feelings and Attitudes in the Poem

1)   The poet is <u>frightened</u> by what's happening, but <u>admires</u> his mum's courage.

2)   There's a sense of <u>panic</u> in the villagers' reactions. Even his dad,
who <u>isn't religious</u>, goes along with the religious stuff (lines 36-40).

3)   The poet doesn't seem impressed by <u>religion</u> — the ceremonial language
and all that talk of the next life seem <u>unhelpful</u> and <u>premature</u>.

Think About Your Feelings and Attitudes to the Poem

1)   Pick two words or phrases that <u>stand out to you</u>. If none do, just pick two <u>unusual words or phrases</u>.

2)   Write these two words or phrases down. Then write about how they <u>make you feel</u>. If they don't make
you feel anything, don't worry — just <u>make something up</u>, as long as it's <u>not too stupid</u>.

> **EXAMPLE**   The phrase "the flame feeding on my mother" makes me feel very uneasy,
> as it sounds like she's being eaten alive. It seems to me that these 'cures' are actually
> making his mother's suffering worse, rather than reducing it.

Compare the last bit to the rest of the poem

The final three lines of the poem are separated from the rest. This last bit's about his mother's calm,
<u>unselfish reaction</u>. It's separate because it's a clear <u>contrast</u> to the <u>panic</u> of the rest of the poem.
After all, it's only a scorpion, it's not like it's poisonous or summat... Eh? Oh, right.

Chinua Achebe

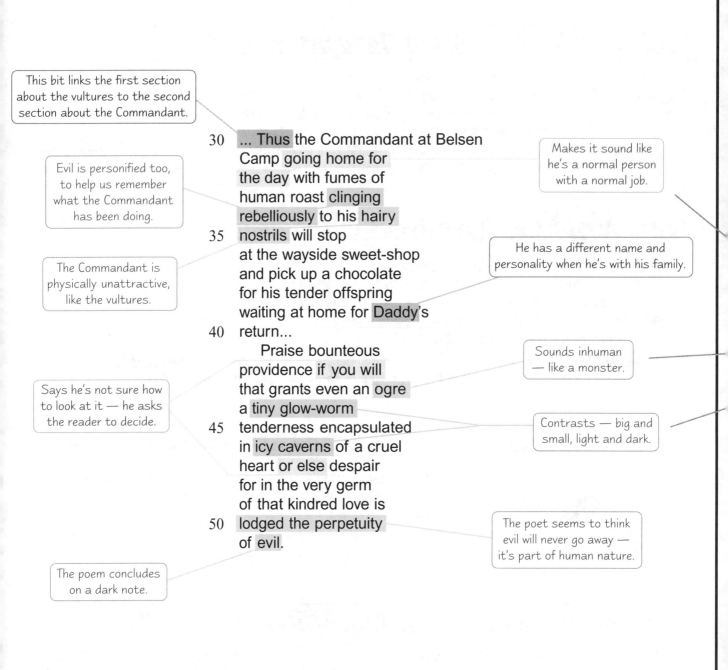

This bit links the first section about the vultures to the second section about the Commandant.

Makes it sound like he's a normal person with a normal job.

Evil is personified too, to help us remember what the Commandant has been doing.

He has a different name and personality when he's with his family.

The Commandant is physically unattractive, like the vultures.

Sounds inhuman — like a monster.

Says he's not sure how to look at it — he asks the reader to decide.

Contrasts — big and small, light and dark.

The poet seems to think evil will never go away — it's part of human nature.

The poem concludes on a dark note.

30   ... Thus the Commandant at Belsen
Camp going home for
the day with fumes of
human roast clinging
rebelliously to his hairy
35   nostrils will stop
at the wayside sweet-shop
and pick up a chocolate
for his tender offspring
waiting at home for Daddy's
40   return...
        Praise bounteous
providence if you will
that grants even an ogre
a tiny glow-worm
45   tenderness encapsulated
in icy caverns of a cruel
heart or else despair
for in the very germ
of that kindred love is
50   lodged the perpetuity
of evil.

POEM DICTIONARY
harbinger — a messenger / a sign of things to come
charnel-house — a place where corpses are stored
Commandant — a commanding officer
Belsen — a Nazi concentration camp in Germany, where people (mostly Jews) were held and killed during World War II
bounteous providence — the good things that God has given to mankind
encapsulated — enclosed
perpetuity — lasting forever

Chinua Achebe

Chinua Achebe was born in Nigeria in 1931. He worked for the Nigerian Broadcasting Corporation, but when war broke out in 1967, he started to work for the government of Biafra (an area that violently split from the rest of Nigeria). He's written lots of poems about war and its effects.

Vultures

All these words are related to darkness and misery. They set the tone of the poem.

In the greyness
and drizzle of one despondent
dawn unstirred by harbingers
of sunbreak a vulture
5   perching high on broken
bone of a dead tree
nestled close to his
mate his smooth
bashed-in head, a pebble
10   on a stem rooted in
a dump of gross
feathers, inclined affectionately
to hers. Yesterday they picked
the eyes of a swollen
15   corpse in a water-logged
trench and ate the
things in its bowel. Full
gorged they chose their roost
keeping the hollowed remnant
20   in easy range of cold
telescopic eyes ...
        Strange
indeed how love in other
ways so particular
25   will pick a corner
in that charnel-house
tidy it and coil up there, perhaps
even fall asleep – her face
turned to the wall!

The vultures live off death.

The vulture's ugliness adds to the evil mood.

Contrasts with the ugliness of the vulture.

Nothing is too disgusting for the vultures.

They see it as an object rather than something that has been alive.

Having this word on its own sounds like he's stopping to think about it.

Personification of love.

The idea of love sleeping among dead bodies is sad and unpleasant.

Love ignores evil.

THIS IS A FLAP.
FOLD THIS PAGE OUT.

Vultures

This poem's pretty grim. We're told how a pair of vultures, despite having some <u>disgusting</u> eating habits, are still capable of <u>affection</u> for each other. The poet compares the vultures to a <u>Nazi officer</u> who's <u>cruel and murderous</u> at work, but <u>loving and kind</u> when he's with his family.

You've Got To Know What Happens in the Poem

<u>Lines 1-21</u>   A pair of <u>vultures</u> are described, scoffing down <u>eyes</u> and stuff. Nice.

<u>Lines 22-29</u>   He discusses how <u>odd</u> it is that love — seen here as a <u>person</u> — chooses to <u>ignore</u> the presence of evil.

<u>Lines 30-40</u>   A <u>Nazi commandant</u> goes home, with the smell of <u>murder</u> clinging to him (lines 32-35). He buys some <u>sweets</u> for his child/ren waiting for him at home (lines 37-38).

<u>Lines 41-51</u>   The poet finishes by saying you could look at it <u>two ways</u>: on the one hand you could be <u>grateful</u> that such an <u>evil</u> person even has a <u>shred of decency</u> in him (lines 41-47)... on the other hand, the good inside that person will always be <u>infected with evil</u> (lines 47-51).

Learn About the Three Types of Language

1) <u>CONTEMPLATIVE TONE</u> — although the poet talks about disgusting things, he <u>doesn't</u> seem <u>shocked</u> by them. He <u>thinks about</u> human evil, and how love can't defeat cruelty — he says it's "Strange" (line 22), rather than tragic.

2) <u>EVIL MOOD</u> — the poem starts at dawn, but there's <u>no sign of the sun</u> (lines 3-4). There are loads of words related to <u>darkness</u>, <u>death</u> and <u>ugliness</u> — a sad and grim mood hangs over the poem.

3) <u>METAPHORICAL LANGUAGE</u> — the <u>vultures</u> are compared to evil people. There's a lot of <u>symbolism</u> — love is seen as a <u>person</u>, who chooses not to notice the less pleasant aspects of humanity (lines 22-29).

Remember the Feelings and Attitudes in the Poem

Who's a pretty boy then?

1) The poet finds the appearance and behaviour of the vultures (lines 8-21) and the Commandant (30-35) <u>unpleasant</u>.

2) But he's <u>not shocked</u> by it. He tries to understand it.

3) He's <u>unsure</u> about how to look at the fact that people are capable of both kindness and cruelty (41-51).

Think About Your Feelings and Attitudes to the Poem

1) Pick two words or phrases that <u>stand out to you</u>. If none do, just pick two <u>unusual words or phrases</u>.

2) Write these two words or phrases down. Then write about how they <u>make you feel</u>. If they don't make you feel anything, don't worry — just <u>make something up</u>, as long as it's <u>not too stupid</u>.

> EXAMPLE   The phrase "a tiny glow-worm / tenderness" makes me feel very depressed. Although good exists in the Commandant, it seems so insignificant when compared to the "icy caverns" of cruelty — it seems impossible that goodness will come out on top.

The link between the vultures and the man is crucial

The stuff about vultures, even though there's a lot of it, is there mainly as a way of <u>introducing</u> the topic of good and evil in <u>people</u>, or as a metaphor for the Nazi Commandant. It's as if the poet's seen the vultures feeding, and it's <u>reminded</u> him of the fact that people can do dreadful things.

Denise Levertov

Denise Levertov (1923-97) was born in England but moved to New York in 1947. She later became an American citizen, but was strongly opposed to the USA's involvement in the Vietnam War.

The poet uses the Vietnamese spelling, rather than the Western version — she sees things from their point of view.

The questions are all in the past tense — this way of life is a thing of the past.

What Were They Like?

1) Did the people of Viet Nam
   use lanterns of stone?
2) Did they hold ceremonies
   to reverence the opening of buds?
3) Were they inclined to quiet laughter?
4) Did they use bone and ivory,
   jade and silver, for ornament?
5) Had they an epic poem?
6) Did they distinguish between speech and singing?

Shows Vietnamese people's respect for nature, and the simplicity of their lifestyle.

They seem modest and gentle.

Vietnamese is a tonal language — it sounds song-like.

Sounds like a military investigation.

Answers are cautious and uncertain.

A brutal and bleak way of tracking time.

A poetic but vague way of measuring time.

1) Sir, their light hearts turned to stone.
   It is not remembered whether in gardens
   stone lanterns illumined pleasant ways.
2) Perhaps they gathered once to delight in blossom,
   but after the children were killed
   there were no more buds)
3) Sir, laughter is bitter to the burned mouth.
4) A dream ago, perhaps. Ornament is for joy.
   All the bones were charred.
5) It is not remembered. Remember,
   most were peasants; their life
   was in rice and bamboo.
   When peaceful clouds were reflected in the paddies
   and the water buffalo stepped surely along terraces,
   maybe fathers told their sons old tales.
   When bombs smashed those mirrors
   there was time only to scream.
6) There is an echo yet
   of their speech which was like a song.
   It was reported that their singing resembled
   the flight of moths in moonlight.
   Who can say? It is silent now.

Their hearts have been hardened.

Seems uncaring and unemotional.

The alliteration reinforces the horror of the bombing, which burnt all in its path.

The meaning of "bone" has changed from in the question.

They lived simple, peaceful lives — this makes the war seem even more barbaric.

The shocking violence of these 2 lines shatters the peace of the previous 6 lines about life before the war.

Sounds distant.

Before the war, they felt safe and confident.

i.e. The paddy fields.

Suggests the soft, gentle beauty of their language.

The answers conclude with a question — they haven't really answered anything.

The culture seems lost for ever.

POEM DICTIONARY

reverence — deep respect or worship
illumined — lit up
paddies — waterlogged fields for growing rice

jade — a gemstone, normally green
charred — blackened by fire
terraces — different levels of fields for farming

What Were They Like?

This poem is written as though Vietnamese culture is a thing of the past and someone is trying to find out about it. They ask six questions but the answers reveal that the devastation caused by the war has removed all traces of the culture.

You've Got To Know What Happens in the Poem

Verse 1 — This is a series of <u>questions</u> about how Vietnamese people used to live before the war. It asks about their <u>way of life</u> (Questions 1 and 4), their <u>culture</u> (Questions 2 and 5), their <u>behaviour</u> (Question 3), and their <u>language</u> (Question 6).

Verse 2 — This <u>answers</u> the questions one by one. We're told that they used to be light-hearted and happy, but the war <u>changed</u> that (Answers 1 and 3). Their <u>history is lost</u> and their <u>culture destroyed</u>, and there are references to the violence and horror of this destruction (Answers 2, 4 and 5). The uncertain tone of the answers suggests the person speaking them <u>can't remember</u> life before the war (Answer 6).

Learn About the Four Types of Language

1) <u>RESPECTFUL LANGUAGE</u> — the poet sees the Vietnamese people and culture as <u>beautiful</u> and <u>simple</u> (e.g. Answer 5). This makes the destruction caused by the war seem even worse.

2) <u>METAPHORICAL LANGUAGE</u> — there's a <u>mythical</u> feel to some of the language (e.g. Answer 5). This is related to the <u>old stories</u> and <u>ceremonies</u> of the Vietnamese culture.

3) <u>FORMAL TONE</u> — it's based around the style of a formal <u>military investigation</u>. Answers 1 and 3 start with "Sir" — like a soldier reporting back to his superior officer.

4) <u>SENSE OF DEVASTATION</u> — <u>war</u> and <u>destruction</u> are constant themes. The whole poem is in the past tense, suggesting that everything that's being described has been <u>lost for ever</u>.

Remember the Feelings and Attitudes in the Poem

A paddy field

1) On the surface of it, the tone is <u>formal</u> and <u>unemotional</u> (e.g. Question 1).

2) But really the poet is <u>sad</u> at what has happened, and <u>angry</u> at those responsible (Answers 3 and 4). She criticises the <u>thoughtlessness</u> of the war.

3) There's a sense of <u>regret</u> at what has been lost (Answer 6).

Think About Your Feelings and Attitudes to the Poem

1) Pick two words or phrases that <u>stand out to you</u>. If none do, just pick two <u>unusual words or phrases</u>.

2) Write these two words or phrases down. Then write about how they <u>make you feel</u>. If they don't make you feel anything, don't worry — just <u>make something up</u>, as long as it's <u>not too stupid</u>.

> **EXAMPLE** The phrase, "It is silent now", at the end of the poem, makes me feel desperately sad, because it seems that the war has completely destroyed this beautiful culture.

Match each answer to its question

You might find it useful to tackle the poem by reading one <u>question</u>, then the <u>matching answer</u> — this way, you can see how the use of one word <u>changes</u> between the question and the answer, e.g. "stone" in Q1 and A1. Also, reading up on the background to the <u>Vietnam War</u> will help loads.

Sujata Bhatt

Sujata Bhatt was born in India in 1956, later lived in the USA and now lives in Germany. She writes in both English and Gujarati, her mother tongue.

from Search For My Tongue

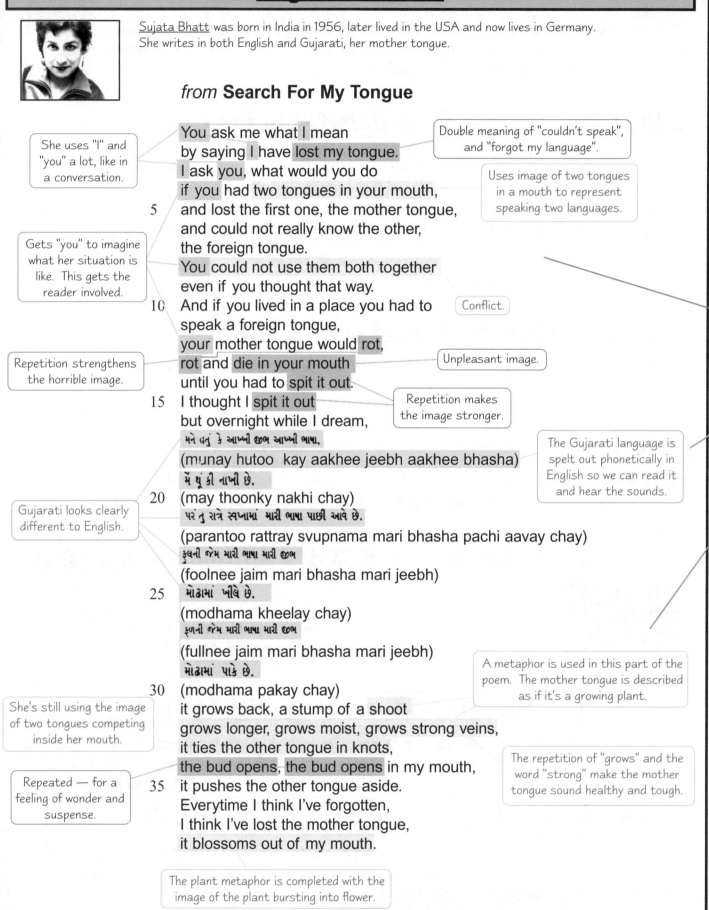

She uses "I" and "you" a lot, like in a conversation.

> You ask me what I mean
> by saying I have lost my tongue.
> I ask you, what would you do

Double meaning of "couldn't speak", and "forgot my language".

Uses image of two tongues in a mouth to represent speaking two languages.

> if you had two tongues in your mouth,
> 5   and lost the first one, the mother tongue,
> and could not really know the other,
> the foreign tongue.

Gets "you" to imagine what her situation is like. This gets the reader involved.

> You could not use them both together
> even if you thought that way.
> 10   And if you lived in a place you had to
> speak a foreign tongue,

Conflict.

> your mother tongue would rot,
> rot and die in your mouth

Repetition strengthens the horrible image.

Unpleasant image.

> until you had to spit it out.
> 15   I thought I spit it out
> but overnight while I dream,

Repetition makes the image stronger.

> મને હતું કે આખ્ખી જીભ આખ્ખી ભાષા,
> (munay hutoo kay aakhee jeebh aakhee bhasha)
> મેં થૂંકી નાખી છે.
> 20   (may thoonky nakhi chay)

The Gujarati language is spelt out phonetically in English so we can read it and hear the sounds.

Gujarati looks clearly different to English.

> પરંતુ રાત્રે સ્વપ્નામાં મારી ભાષા પાછી આવે છે.
> (parantoo rattray svupnama mari bhasha pachi aavay chay)
> ફૂલની જેમ મારી ભાષા મારી જીભ
> (foolnee jaim mari bhasha mari jeebh)
> 25   મોઢામાં ખીલે છે.
> (modhama kheelay chay)
> ફૂલની જેમ મારી ભાષા મારી જીભ
> (fullnee jaim mari bhasha mari jeebh)
> મોઢામાં પાકે છે.

A metaphor is used in this part of the poem. The mother tongue is described as if it's a growing plant.

She's still using the image of two tongues competing inside her mouth.

> 30   (modhama pakay chay)
> it grows back, a stump of a shoot
> grows longer, grows moist, grows strong veins,
> it ties the other tongue in knots,
> the bud opens, the bud opens in my mouth,

The repetition of "grows" and the word "strong" make the mother tongue sound healthy and tough.

Repeated — for a feeling of wonder and suspense.

> 35   it pushes the other tongue aside.
> Everytime I think I've forgotten,
> I think I've lost the mother tongue,
> it blossoms out of my mouth.

The plant metaphor is completed with the image of the plant bursting into flower.

POEM DICTIONARY
mother tongue — a person's first language

Search For My Tongue

This poem is about the <u>conflict</u> between the poet's first language and the foreign language she now uses. The poet is really <u>worried</u> she'll <u>forget her first language</u> (mother tongue), but it turns out all right in the end — her mother tongue is always with her in her dreams. Ahhhhh...

You've Got To Know the Structure of the Poem

Lines 1-15   Explain the <u>problem</u> she has of being <u>fluent in two languages</u>. She uses the image of having "two tongues in your mouth" to explain what it is like.

Lines 16-30   When she's asleep she <u>dreams in her mother tongue</u>. This is in the middle of the poem because it's the centre of her problems.

Lines 31-38   Describe how her <u>mother tongue grows back</u> every time she thinks she has forgotten it — it is stronger and "pushes the other tongue aside" (line 35).

Learn About the Three Types of Language

1) <u>CONVERSATIONAL LANGUAGE</u> — in the first part of the poem, the poet uses chatty language (e.g. "I ask you", line 3). It makes it sound like she's <u>talking to the reader</u> about her problem.

2) <u>FOREIGN LANGUAGE</u> — in the middle part of the poem, there is <u>Gujarati</u> language. This shows us her mother tongue <u>visually</u>, and emphasises its difference from English.

3) <u>METAPHORICAL LANGUAGE</u> — In the last part of the poem she uses more <u>poetic</u> language — very different to the chatty language in the first part of the poem. She uses the <u>metaphor</u> of her mother tongue growing back like a flower.

> **DOUBLE MEANING**
> *"Tongue" can mean both the fleshy thing in your mouth and a language.*

Remember the Feelings and Attitudes in the Poem

1) She <u>worries</u> that she is <u>forgetting her mother tongue</u> — and that her second language will never feel as natural (lines 1-7).

2) This is part of a bigger worry that she might <u>lose her Indian identity</u> by living in another country. She's concerned that she's <u>stuck between different cultures</u> (lines 4-9).

3) She's <u>happy</u> when she realises that her mother tongue will <u>always be a part of her</u> — "it <u>blossoms</u> out of my mouth."

Think About Your Feelings and Attitudes to the Poem

1) Pick two words or phrases that <u>stand out to you</u>. If none do, just pick two <u>unusual words or phrases</u>.

2) Write these two words or phrases down. Then write about how they <u>make you feel</u>. If they don't make you feel anything, don't worry — just <u>make something up</u>, as long as it's not too stupid.

> **EXAMPLE**   On line 38, the poet describes how her mother tongue "blossoms out" of her mouth. I think this image is really beautiful and it makes it seem natural that she'll always remember her first language, even if she worries that she's forgotten it.

This poem is about more than languages...

This poem highlights the difficulties of being part of two cultures — <u>language</u> is an essential part of <u>culture and identity</u>. There's more about identity on page 34 — other poets focus on this topic too.

Tom Leonard

Tom Leonard was born in Glasgow in 1944. He's often written about people's attitudes to different accents, and says he writes in Scottish dialect so that his 'voice' can be heard through his poetry.

© Gordon Wright

from Unrelated Incidents

> The lack of capital letters and speech marks makes it sound informal — like someone's talking.

> Posh English accent.

> "wouldn't want"

> "commoners"

```
   this is thi
   six a clock
   news thi
   man said n
5  thi reason
   a talk wia
   BBC accent
   iz coz yi
   widny wahnt
10 mi ti talk
   aboot thi
   trooth wia
   voice lik
   wanna yoo
15 scruff. if
   a toktaboot
   thi trooth
   lik wanna yoo
   scruff yi
20 widny thingk
   it wuz troo.
   jist wanna yoo
   scruff tokn.
   thirza right
25 way ti spell
   ana right way
   ti tok it. this
   is me tokn yir
   right way a
30 spellin. this
   is ma trooth
   yooz doant no
   thi trooth
   yirsellz cawz
35 yi canny talk
   right. this is
   the six a clock
   nyooz. belt up.
```

> "with a"

> The short lines make the poem look like a newsreader's <u>autocue</u>, scrolling quickly down for easy reading. They also add to the <u>abrupt</u>, no-nonsense feel of the dialect.

> "talked about"

> Says that even people with regional accents don't want to hear the news read in one.

> Sounds very disrespectful towards working-class people.

> The newsreader sees regional accents as "the wrong way".

> Non-standard spelling of the word "spellin" is funny and underlines his idea that there isn't really a right way and a wrong way to speak and write.

> People from different social classes have their own ideas of the truth.

> "you can't"

> He copies the newsreader's posh accent in this last bit.

> Working-class people are denied the chance to have their voices heard on the news.

Unrelated Incidents

This poem's about people's attitudes towards <u>accents</u>. The poet imagines a newsreader saying that the news has got to be read in a <u>posh accent</u>, because if it was read in a working-class, regional accent, no one would take it seriously. Confusingly, all this is described in <u>Scottish dialect</u>.

You've Got To Know What Happens in the Poem

<u>Lines 1-15</u>   The poet <u>imagines</u> a newsreader saying to him, "I talk with a <u>posh accent</u> because no one wants to hear the news read in a <u>common</u> accent like <u>yours</u>."

<u>Lines 15-23</u>   "If I talked like you, you <u>wouldn't think it was true</u> — you'd think it was just one of you commoners talking."

<u>Lines 24-30</u>   "There's a <u>right way</u> to spell and talk. I'm talking the right way."

<u>Lines 30-38</u>   "This is <u>my</u> truth. You don't know the truth because you <u>can't talk right</u>. Shut up."

Learn About the Two Types of Language

1)   <u>SCOTTISH ACCENT and DIALECT</u> — the words are spelt <u>phonetically</u>, i.e. they're spelt like they sound. This is important as he's attacking people who <u>don't value accents</u> — he's trying to make them <u>re-think</u> their ideas.

2)   <u>POLITICAL LANGUAGE</u> — accents are linked to <u>class</u>. The poet says that <u>working-class</u> people are <u>denied</u> the chance to use their own voice (32-38). When they listen to the news, it's a <u>posh English</u> person telling them the "trooth".

> **ACCENT AND DIALECT**
>
> <u>Accent</u> means the way people pronounce certain words.
> <u>Dialect</u> means the words and grammar a person uses, and their accent.

Remember the Feelings and Attitudes in the Poem

Not all Scottish people look like this.

1)   He's <u>annoyed</u> at the dominance of posh, English accents in the media, and about how working-class, regional accents are not heard.

2)   He <u>mocks</u> the idea of snobby people looking down on regional accents as <u>inferior</u> (35-36).

3)   He criticises this snobbery in a <u>sarcastic</u> way, by "translating" it into his own dialect.

4)   What he's getting at overall is that you <u>shouldn't judge</u> people by the way they talk.

Think About Your Feelings and Attitudes to the Poem

1)   Pick two words or phrases that <u>stand out to you</u>. If none do, just pick two <u>unusual words or phrases</u>.

2)   Write these two words or phrases down. Then write about how they <u>make you feel</u>. If they don't make you feel anything, don't worry — just <u>make something up</u>, as long as it's <u>not too stupid</u>.

> **EXAMPLE**   The phrase "wanna yoo / scruff" makes me annoyed at the arrogance of the newsreader. He seems to look down on people with regional accents just because of the way they talk.

Think about how the poem sounds when it's spoken

Most of the poem's written in <u>dialect</u>, which can make it a tad <u>tricky to understand</u> if you're not used to it. Try to 'hear' it in your head — or even read it out loud — then imagine the bloke out of <u>Taggart</u> saying it. An uf thaht disnae help, muv tae Scoatland fer a bit, ye moanin Sassenach.

22

John Agard

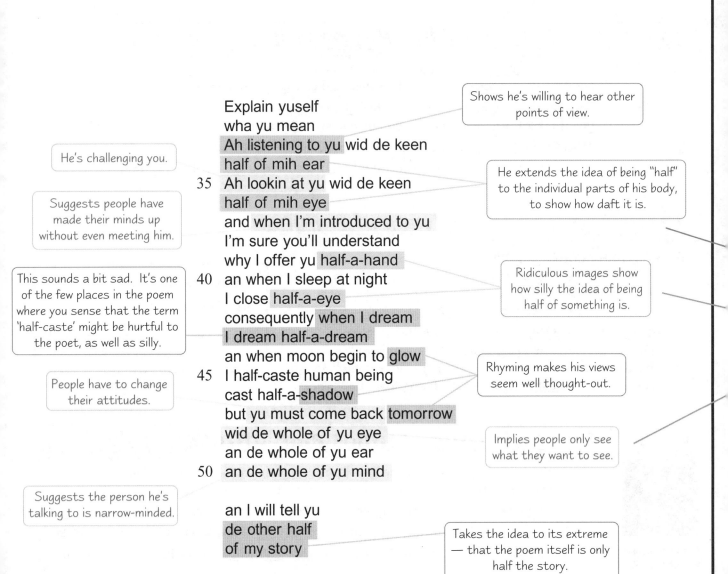

Shows he's willing to hear other points of view.

He's challenging you.

Suggests people have made their minds up without even meeting him.

This sounds a bit sad. It's one of the few places in the poem where you sense that the term 'half-caste' might be hurtful to the poet, as well as silly.

People have to change their attitudes.

Suggests the person he's talking to is narrow-minded.

Explain yuself
wha yu mean
Ah listening to yu wid de keen
half of mih ear
35   Ah lookin at yu wid de keen
half of mih eye
and when I'm introduced to yu
I'm sure you'll understand
why I offer yu half-a-hand
40   an when I sleep at night
I close half-a-eye
consequently when I dream
I dream half-a-dream
an when moon begin to glow
45   I half-caste human being
cast half-a-shadow
but yu must come back tomorrow
wid de whole of yu eye
an de whole of yu ear
50   an de whole of yu mind

an I will tell yu
de other half
of my story

He extends the idea of being "half" to the individual parts of his body, to show how daft it is.

Ridiculous images show how silly the idea of being half of something is.

Rhyming makes his views seem well thought-out.

Implies people only see what they want to see.

Takes the idea to its extreme — that the poem itself is only half the story.

POEM DICTIONARY
Picasso — the name of a 20th Century Spanish artist
Tchaikovsky — the name of a 19th Century Russian classical music composer
half-caste — an old-fashioned term for a person with parents of different races, today often considered to be offensive

John Agard

John Agard was born in Guyana in South America in 1949, to parents of mixed nationality. He came to Britain in 1977. He likes to perform his poems, and believes humour is a good way of challenging people's opinions.

Half-Caste

Excuse me
standing on one leg
I'm half-caste

> Introduces the subject in a jokey way, poking fun at the term "half-caste".

> It sounds like he's talking to the reader, but in a slightly aggressive way — this bit of the poem is repeated several times.

5   Explain yuself
wha yu mean
when yu say half-caste
yu mean when picasso
mix red an green
is a half-caste canvas/

> He compares having parents of different colour to mixing the colours of a great painting.

10 explain yuself
wha yu mean
when yu say half-caste
yu mean when light an shadow
mix in de sky

> Natural image — shows there's nothing wrong with colours mixing.

> He uses a chatty but challenging tone.

15 is a half-caste weather/
well in dat case
england weather
nearly always half-caste
in fact some o dem cloud

> Plays with the double meaning of cast/caste.

> His use of creole, mixed in with standard English, shows he's comfortable with the different sides to his background. He's also showing you how the poem might sound if he was saying the words, which emphasises the conversational style.

20 half-caste till dem overcast
so spiteful dem dont want de sun pass
ah rass/
explain yuself
wha yu mean
25 when yu say half-caste
yu mean tchaikovsky
sit down at dah piano
an mix a black key
wid a white key
30 is a half-caste symphony/

> He says we wouldn't have had great music without mixing colours together.

> Piano music uses a mixture of black and white keys, but people don't call it half-caste — so why are people who are part black and part white described like that?

Section One — The Poems

THIS IS A FLAP.
FOLD THIS PAGE OUT.

Half-Caste

The poet makes fun of the term "half-caste" (someone with parents of different races). He sees himself as being a <u>mix</u> of things — rather than <u>half</u> of something — and compares it to loads of other things which are great because they're made up of mixtures, like <u>paintings</u> and <u>symphonies</u>.

You've Got To Know What Happens in the Poem

<u>Lines 1-30</u>   The poet asks what the term "half-caste" is supposed to <u>mean</u>. He says if you look at things like that, then everything that's <u>mixed</u> could be called half-caste, like great <u>paintings</u> (lines 6-9), the <u>weather</u> (13-15), and <u>classical music</u> (26-30).

<u>Lines 31-53</u>   He <u>challenges</u> people to explain their way of thinking, but finds no logic in it. He <u>mocks</u> the idea by talking about "halves" of other things, e.g. line 34. He says people should <u>sort their ideas out</u>, by opening their eyes and their minds.

Learn About the Three Types of Language

1)   <u>METAPHORICAL LANGUAGE</u> — he compares being of mixed race to the different colours of a <u>painting</u>, showing it's <u>beautiful</u>, and to the <u>weather</u>, showing it's <u>natural</u>. This is central to his argument against the term "half-caste", which he sees as <u>negative</u>.

2)   <u>HUMOUR</u> — he makes the idea of being "half" of something <u>laughable</u>. He <u>mocks</u> the people who use the word by making it sound ridiculous (e.g. line 39).

3)   <u>ARGUMENTATIVE TONE</u> — the style is <u>conversational</u> — "yu" and "I" are used a lot — but also <u>confrontational</u>. He challenges the reader by repeatedly saying "Explain yuself" (lines 4, 10, 23, 31). He uses Caribbean <u>creole</u> (dialect) and <u>no punctuation</u>, which makes it sound direct and informal.

Remember the Feelings and Attitudes in the Poem

Half a horse

1)   He <u>mocks</u> the idea of mixed-race people being inferior or "incomplete".

2)   He's <u>baffled</u> and <u>amused</u> by the idea of being half a person.

3)   He gets <u>angry</u> that some people aren't more open-minded, and he <u>tells them off</u> at the end (47-50).

4)   The last three lines of the poem sound more <u>forgiving</u> — he's still prepared to talk to these people if they're <u>willing to listen</u>. This shows that the real point of the poem is to <u>encourage</u> others to <u>think about their attitudes</u> towards people of mixed race.

Think About Your Feelings and Attitudes to the Poem

1)   Pick two words or phrases that <u>stand out to you</u>. If none do, just pick two <u>unusual words or phrases</u>.

2)   Write these two words or phrases down. Then write about how they <u>make you feel</u>. If they don't make you feel anything, don't worry — just <u>make something up</u>, as long as it's <u>not too stupid</u>.

> EXAMPLE   The phrase "half-a-hand" seems funny and absurd. It's a bizarre image, and just shows how ridiculous it is to use the word "half-caste" to describe a person.

The jokes are crucial to the point being made

A good way to pick up marks here is to talk about <u>how</u> the humour helps the poet <u>make his point</u>. It's not good enough just to say it's funny — you have to <u>work out</u> what he's actually getting at.

Derek Walcott

Derek Walcott was born in St Lucia, in the West Indies, in 1930.
His father was English and his mother was African.
As well as poetry, he's written plays and is a painter.

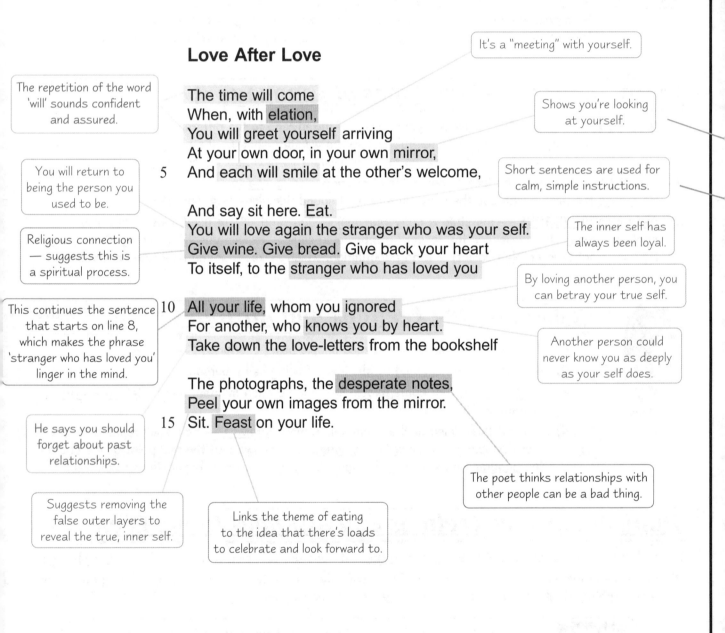

Love After Love

It's a "meeting" with yourself.

The repetition of the word 'will' sounds confident and assured.

The time will come
When, with elation,
You will greet yourself arriving
At your own door, in your own mirror,
5   And each will smile at the other's welcome,

Shows you're looking at yourself.

Short sentences are used for calm, simple instructions.

You will return to being the person you used to be.

And say sit here. Eat.
You will love again the stranger who was your self.
Give wine. Give bread. Give back your heart
To itself, to the stranger who has loved you

The inner self has always been loyal.

Religious connection — suggests this is a spiritual process.

By loving another person, you can betray your true self.

This continues the sentence that starts on line 8, which makes the phrase 'stranger who has loved you' linger in the mind.

10   All your life, whom you ignored
For another, who knows you by heart.
Take down the love-letters from the bookshelf

Another person could never know you as deeply as your self does.

He says you should forget about past relationships.

The photographs, the desperate notes,
Peel your own images from the mirror.
15   Sit. Feast on your life.

The poet thinks relationships with other people can be a bad thing.

Suggests removing the false outer layers to reveal the true, inner self.

Links the theme of eating to the idea that there's loads to celebrate and look forward to.

POEM DICTIONARY
Elation — joy and excitement

Love After Love

"Love After Love" is about finding <u>happiness</u> on your own after the end of a relationship.
The poet says that being in love can make you forget who you <u>really are</u>. So beautiful (sniff)...

You've Got To Know What Happens in the Poem

<u>Lines 1-5</u>   The poet says confidently that, after splitting up with someone, you'll eventually return
to your <u>own identity</u> (lines 3-5) — and you'll be <u>happy</u> about it ("with elation", line 2).

<u>Lines 6-11</u>   There are offerings of <u>food and drink</u> (line 8) — it's a <u>celebration</u>. He says you should
get to know your "self" again, as you know yourself better than any other person (line 11).

<u>Lines 12-15</u> He suggests <u>removing</u> all the signs of previous relationships, like <u>photos</u> and stuff (12-13).
Just chill out and <u>make the most</u> of your life (line 15).

Learn About the Three Types of Language

1) <u>CEREMONIAL LANGUAGE</u> — there are <u>religious</u> references (line 8), and at times it sounds
like a religious ceremony (lines 8 and 15), marking a <u>new start in life</u>.

2) <u>REFERENCES TO THE "SELF"</u> — the "self" is seen as more than just an identity — it's a
person <u>within you</u>. The message of the poem is that you <u>neglect</u> this self when you love
another person ("whom you ignored", line 10), so you should <u>get to know it</u> again.

3) <u>INSTRUCTIVE LANGUAGE</u> — the style is like a <u>self-help</u> book. It's <u>advice</u> that the poet wants to
pass down. There's no "maybe" or "possibly" about it — these things <u>will</u> happen (e.g. line 1).

Remember the Feelings and Attitudes in the Poem

Cheers.
Here's to me.

1) He's <u>positive</u> and <u>optimistic</u>. He says it's good to have time
to get to know yourself again. He thinks you'll be <u>better off</u>
this way than you would be living with someone else.

2) There's a <u>calm confidence</u> in the advice the poet gives.
It's based on his own experiences, and he seems <u>certain</u>
that what he's saying is good advice.

Think About Your Feelings and Attitudes to the Poem

1) Pick two words or phrases that <u>stand out to you</u>. If none do, just pick two <u>unusual words or phrases</u>.

2) Write these two words or phrases down. Then write about how they <u>make you feel</u>. If they don't
make you feel anything, don't worry — just <u>make something up</u>, as long as it's <u>not too stupid</u>.

> **EXAMPLE**   One piece of advice that particularly stands out is, "Give back your heart /
> To itself". The suggestion that a lover can steal your heart, and that you should claim
> it back, seems to sum up the poet's negative feelings about past relationships.

Exam After Exam

The day will come when, with reluctance, you must face an exam. You will greet your teacher,
arriving in the Sports Hall. And he will say, "Sit here. Write your name on the front of the paper.
Take pens. Take pencils. Give back all revision materials. Sit. Feast on your exam."

Imtiaz Dharker

Imtiaz Dharker was born in 1954 in Pakistan. She has said that she believes identity comes from "beliefs and states of mind", rather than nationality or religion.

This Room

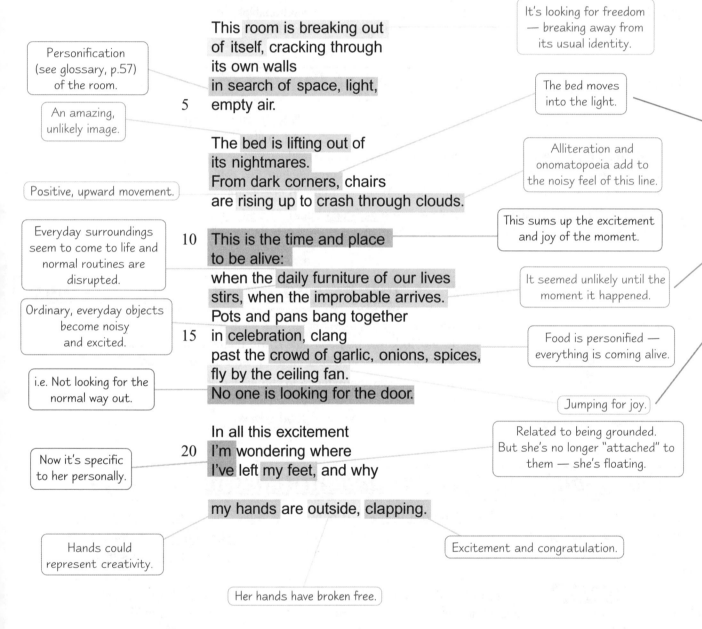

This room is breaking out
of itself, cracking through
its own walls
in search of space, light,
5   empty air.

The bed is lifting out of
its nightmares.
From dark corners, chairs
are rising up to crash through clouds.

10   This is the time and place
to be alive:
when the daily furniture of our lives
stirs, when the improbable arrives.
Pots and pans bang together
15   in celebration, clang
past the crowd of garlic, onions, spices,
fly by the ceiling fan.
No one is looking for the door.

In all this excitement
20   I'm wondering where
I've left my feet, and why

my hands are outside, clapping.

Annotations:

Personification (see glossary, p.57) of the room.

An amazing, unlikely image.

Positive, upward movement.

Everyday surroundings seem to come to life and normal routines are disrupted.

Ordinary, everyday objects become noisy and excited.

i.e. Not looking for the normal way out.

Now it's specific to her personally.

Hands could represent creativity.

It's looking for freedom — breaking away from its usual identity.

The bed moves into the light.

Alliteration and onomatopoeia add to the noisy feel of this line.

This sums up the excitement and joy of the moment.

It seemed unlikely until the moment it happened.

Food is personified — everything is coming alive.

Jumping for joy.

Related to being grounded. But she's no longer "attached" to them — she's floating.

Excitement and congratulation.

Her hands have broken free.

POEM DICTIONARY
improbable — unlikely

This Room

"This Room" is about a <u>special event</u> going on in the poet's life, which sets her free from the boredom of everyday life. She <u>rises out</u> of normality and darkness, and the strange event <u>lights up</u> her life.

You've Got To Know What Happens in the Poem

<u>Lines 1-9</u>   The room breaks out of itself, looking for <u>light and freedom</u> (lines 1-5). Then the <u>bed</u> rises into the <u>sky</u>. The <u>chairs</u> clearly reckon this is a smart idea so they get in on the act too.

<u>Lines 10-18</u>   The poet says <u>how great it feels</u> when something that seems really <u>unlikely</u> suddenly happens (lines 10-13). <u>Everyday objects</u> like kitchen utensils and food <u>come alive</u> and make loads of noise to celebrate (lines 14-15).

<u>Lines 19-22</u>   It's all been such <u>fun</u> she feels that she's left her <u>feet</u> behind her, and her newly-freed <u>hands</u> are applauding her.

Learn About the Three Types of Language

1)   <u>PERSONIFICATION</u> — everyday objects come to life (lines 1-9 and 14-17), showing how exciting life has become. Parts of her <u>body</u> move separately from each other (20-22), showing she's become <u>free</u>.

2)   <u>IMPROBABILITY</u> — whatever the event is, it clearly seemed very <u>unlikely</u> right until the moment it happened (line 13). This creates the feeling that there's a <u>sudden explosion</u> of happiness.

3)   <u>MOVEMENT</u> — things move <u>upwards</u> (lines 9 and 17) and expand <u>outwards</u> (2-3), to show how much <u>richer</u> and full of <u>variety</u> life suddenly is. There's a sense of escaping by being <u>outside</u> her body (line 21).

Remember the Feelings and Attitudes in the Poem

1)   She's <u>excited</u> (line 19) about the special moment in her life when things suddenly change for the better (lines 10-11).

2)   She feels <u>joyful</u> and <u>overwhelmed</u> because it's all so sudden and <u>improbable</u> (lines 12-13).

3)   She's <u>relieved</u> that she's suddenly free (line 22).

Think About Your Feelings and Attitudes to the Poem

1)   Pick two words or phrases that <u>stand out to you</u>. If none do, just pick two <u>unusual words or phrases</u>.

2)   Write these two words or phrases down. Then write about how they <u>make you feel</u>. If they don't make you feel anything, don't worry — just <u>make something up</u>, as long as it's <u>not too stupid</u>.

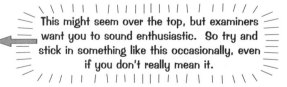

EXAMPLE When the poet says "This is the time and place / to be alive", I'm filled with optimism. It makes me realise that anything is possible, right here and now.

This might seem over the top, but examiners want you to sound enthusiastic. So try and stick in something like this occasionally, even if you don't really mean it.

You have to use your imagination

Well, it's nice to have a <u>cheery</u> poem for a change eh? But what makes this one tricky is that it's <u>not specific</u> about what it's all about — it's just generally about something pretty cool going on. So you can be imaginative — think of an <u>event in your life</u> and relate it to the poem.

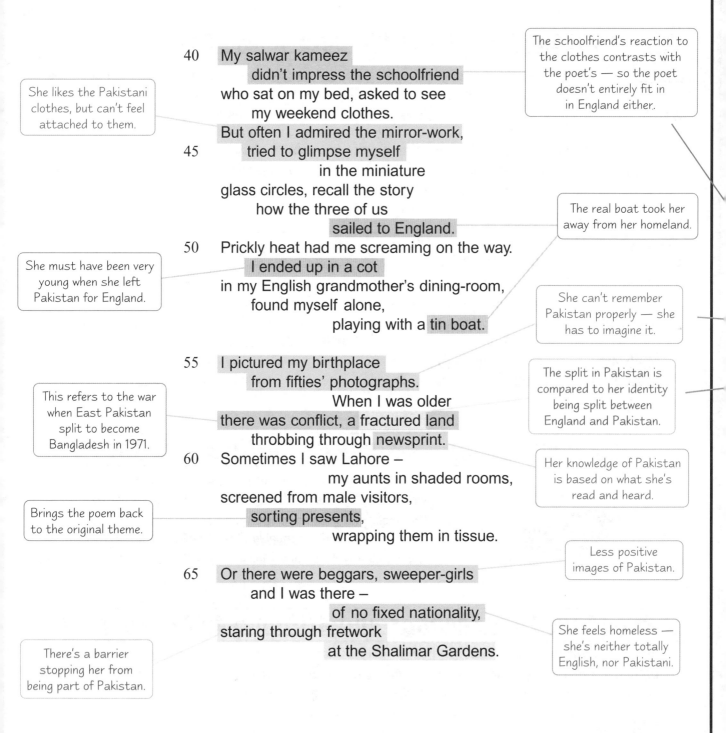

Moniza Alvi

She likes the Pakistani clothes, but can't feel attached to them.

The schoolfriend's reaction to the clothes contrasts with the poet's — so the poet doesn't entirely fit in in England either.

40 My salwar kameez
   didn't impress the schoolfriend
who sat on my bed, asked to see
  my weekend clothes.
But often I admired the mirror-work,
45   tried to glimpse myself
    in the miniature
glass circles, recall the story
  how the three of us
    sailed to England.

The real boat took her away from her homeland.

She must have been very young when she left Pakistan for England.

50 Prickly heat had me screaming on the way.
  I ended up in a cot
in my English grandmother's dining-room,
  found myself alone,
    playing with a tin boat.

She can't remember Pakistan properly — she has to imagine it.

55 I pictured my birthplace
  from fifties' photographs.
    When I was older
there was conflict, a fractured land
  throbbing through newsprint.

The split in Pakistan is compared to her identity being split between England and Pakistan.

This refers to the war when East Pakistan split to become Bangladesh in 1971.

60 Sometimes I saw Lahore –
   my aunts in shaded rooms,
screened from male visitors,
  sorting presents,
    wrapping them in tissue.

Her knowledge of Pakistan is based on what she's read and heard.

Brings the poem back to the original theme.

Less positive images of Pakistan.

65 Or there were beggars, sweeper-girls
  and I was there –
    of no fixed nationality,
staring through fretwork
    at the Shalimar Gardens.

She feels homeless — she's neither totally English, nor Pakistani.

There's a barrier stopping her from being part of Pakistan.

POEM DICTIONARY
salwar kameez — Pakistani items of clothing
filigree — delicate gold jewellery
mirror-work — a way of decorating clothing using little mirrors
Lahore — a city in Pakistan
fretwork — decorative carving or pattern, for example in a gate or wall.
Shalimar Gardens — peaceful, walled gardens in Lahore

Moniza Alvi

Moniza Alvi was born in Pakistan in 1954, to a Pakistani father and an English mother. She moved to England as a child, and revisited Pakistan for the first time in 1993.

Presents from my Aunts in Pakistan

The words for the Pakistani clothes stand out from the English words, just as the presents do from the English clothes she usually wears.

They sent me a salwar kameez
                    peacock-blue,
                              and another
           glistening like an orange split open,
5   embossed slippers, gold and black
                    points curling.

The bright colours of the Pakistani clothes contrast with the clothes she's used to (line 21).

They broke — like her contact with Pakistan.

           Candy-striped glass bangles
                    snapped, drew blood.
           Like at school, fashions changed
10   in Pakistan –
      the salwar bottoms were broad and stiff,
                    then narrow.
      My aunts chose an apple-green sari,
           silver-bordered
15   for my teens.

The presents make her feel out of place in England.

      I tried each satin-silken top –
           was alien in the sitting-room.
      I could never be as lovely
                    as those clothes –
20   I longed
      for denim and corduroy.

She's more comfortable with the plainness of English clothes than the bright colours of the salwar kameez.

She yearns for something she can't have.

           My costume clung to me
                    and I was aflame,
      I couldn't rise up out of its fire,
25   half-English,
                    unlike Aunt Jamila.

Refers to the legend of the Phoenix rising from the flames — but she can't re-create herself like this.

      I wanted my parents' camel-skin lamp –
           switching it on in my bedroom,
      to consider the cruelty
30   and the transformation
      from camel to shade,
           marvel at the colours
                    like stained glass.

She finds the lamp beautiful.

      My mother cherished her jewellery –
35   Indian gold, dangling, filigree.
                    But it was stolen from our car.
      The presents were radiant in my wardrobe.
           My aunts requested cardigans
                    from Marks and Spencers.

Her mother has lost some of her links with Pakistan too.

Humorous and ironic (see glossary, p. 56) — her aunts want stereotypically English things, but she doesn't want stereotypically Pakistani things.

THIS IS A FLAP.
FOLD THIS PAGE OUT.

Presents from my Aunts in Pakistan

A teenage girl who's grown up in England describes the <u>presents</u> she's received from relatives in Pakistan. Despite thinking the clothes and jewellery are <u>beautiful</u>, she feels <u>uncomfortable</u> wearing them. This makes her start thinking about Pakistan and wondering about her <u>mixed identity</u>.

You've Got To Know What Happens in the Poem

<u>Lines 1-26</u>   The poet remembers the <u>clothes</u> her aunts sent her when she was a teenager. When she tried them on, she didn't feel right in them — she thought they were <u>too nice for her</u> (lines 16-20).

<u>Lines 27-43</u>   She thinks of times when the <u>cultures clashed</u>, like the way she felt when her mum's jewellery was <u>stolen</u>, how the clothes from her aunts were very <u>different</u> from what she usually wore, and how her <u>friend</u> didn't like them.

<u>Lines 44-69</u>   The poet tries to make sense of the <u>vague memories</u> she has of first coming to England (lines 48-54), and of Pakistan (lines 55-65). She seems to think she'll never feel either <u>properly Pakistani</u> or <u>properly English</u>.

Learn About the Three Types of Language

1) <u>CONFLICT</u> — Pakistan and England seem to <u>contrast</u> in every possible way, e.g. the <u>bright colours</u> of the salwar kameez are starkly different to the <u>dull</u> Western clothes she prefers to wear.

2) <u>PAIN and UNCERTAINTY</u> — her <u>lack of knowledge</u> about the country where she was born (lines 55-59) makes it difficult for her to understand her identity. She feels <u>uncomfortable</u> when she tries on the Pakistani clothes (line 17). At the end of the poem, she feels <u>isolated</u> and left out of both cultures.

3) <u>METAPHORICAL LANGUAGE</u> — the poet uses metaphors like the <u>situation</u> in Pakistan (line 58) to reflect her own conflict over not quite fitting in.

Remember the Feelings and Attitudes in the Poem

1) There are memories of feeling <u>confused</u> and <u>out of place</u> as a teenager (lines 16-19).

2) The poet has <u>mixed feelings</u> about the presents and about Pakistan — she finds them <u>attractive</u> and exotic (lines 4-6), but also <u>foreign</u> and strange (line 32).

3) She still feels <u>uncertain of her identity</u> at the end of the poem — she seems to feel like an <u>outsider</u> (lines 67-69).

Think About Your Feelings and Attitudes to the Poem

1) Pick two words or phrases that <u>stand out to you</u>. If none do, just pick two <u>unusual words or phrases</u>.

2) Write these two words or phrases down. Then write about how they <u>make you feel</u>. If they don't make you feel anything, don't worry — just <u>make something up</u>, as long as it's <u>not too stupid</u>.

> **EXAMPLE** When the poet describes herself as "of no fixed nationality", I feel sorry for her, because she's still very uncertain of her identity at the end of the poem. It's easy to empathise when reading this poem because all teenagers have to decide who they are, and we feel for the girl in the poem who has added complications.

Talk about the conflict the poet feels

Phew, this poem's a bit of a long 'un. But that's <u>good</u> because there's loads you can get out of it. Like a lot of the poems, it ends on a bit of an <u>uncertain</u> note, so you could write about <u>why</u> you think she's failed to solve her <u>identity crisis</u>. In fact, I'm certain you should do that. Kind of.

Niyi Osundare

Niyi Osundare was born in Nigeria in 1947, and is a Professor of English. He has often spoken out against military regimes in his home country.

Not my Business

He uses first names — he knows all the people who are being abused.

This line emphasises the brutality of his beating.

They picked Akanni up one morning
Beat him soft like clay
And stuffed him down the belly
Of a waiting jeep.

Personification — the jeep is seen as an animal eating him up.

5   What business of mine is it
So long they don't take the yam
From my savouring mouth?

They violently and noisily disturb the sleeping household.

They came one night
Booted the whole house awake
10 And dragged Danladi out,
Then off to a lengthy absence.

It seems like this kind of thing happens all the time, and at any time of day — they're never safe.

      What business of mine is it
So long they don't take the yam
From my savouring mouth?

He hides behind this excuse for not getting involved.

There's an ironically innocent sound to this — her job hasn't really just disappeared.

15 Chinwe went to work one day
Only to find her job was gone:
No query, no warning, no probe –
Just one neat sack for a stainless record.

They don't have to answer to anyone — they can do what they like.

Chinwe's treatment isn't violent, but it's still horribly unfair.

      What business of mine is it
20   So long they don't take the yam
From my savouring mouth?

The simple, factual tone makes it sound inevitable.

Now they've come for him, and he won't get his yam.

And then one evening
As I sat down to eat my yam
A knock on the door froze my hungry hand.
25 The jeep was waiting on my bewildered lawn
Waiting, waiting in its usual silence.

Use of "the" shows it's the same jeep — so presumably he's in the for the same treatment as Akanni.

Menacing, like a predator.

Personification of the lawn stands for the speaker's own frightened confusion.

POEM DICTIONARY
yam — vegetable similar to a potato

Not my Business

Another rather bleak one, I'm afraid. From the point of view of a <u>Nigerian man</u>, the poet describes how various people in his neighbourhood are <u>mistreated</u>, probably by the secret police or the army. The narrator says that as long as he's left alone, it's <u>none of his business</u>. Then they come for him.

You've Got To Know What Happens in the Poem

<u>Lines 1-14</u>	A man called Akanni is <u>beaten up</u> and bundled into a <u>jeep</u> (lines 1-4). Then another man, Danladi, is <u>taken from his house</u> and isn't seen for ages (lines 8-11). After each incident, the narrator says that, as long as he's OK, he's <u>not getting involved</u> (lines 5-7, 12-14).
<u>Lines 15-21</u>	A woman called Chinwe discovers that she's been <u>sacked for no reason</u> (lines 15-18). Again the narrator says that it's <u>no business of his</u> (lines 19-21).
<u>Lines 22-26</u>	As he sits down to eat, he hears a <u>knock on the door</u>. He's dead <u>scared</u> (line 24). He looks outside and sees the jeep <u>waiting for him</u> (lines 25-26). Uh-oh...

Learn About the Two Types of Language

1) <u>NARRATIVE VOICE</u> — the poet uses the voice of an onlooker who thinks he <u>won't be affected</u> by the violence. This adds to the <u>impact</u> at the end when it <u>does</u> happen to him.

2) <u>VIOLENT LANGUAGE</u> — the brutality of the regime is shown by comparisons with <u>savage animals</u> (lines 3 and 26). The regime can get away with being <u>openly barbaric</u>, because people are so scared of it.

> *The last verse doesn't have the usual lines about not caring — the speaker's voice has been silenced. The poet shows the speaker's attitude is wrong, as no one is safe under this kind of regime.*

Remember the Feelings and Attitudes in the Poem

1) The speaker says that what happens to other people <u>isn't his problem</u>.
2) But he's <u>scared</u> when it looks like the same thing will happen to him (line 24).
3) The way the poet describes the abuses (e.g. lines 2 and 17) shows he's actually very <u>angry</u> about them.
4) The message is that you <u>shouldn't ignore</u> these abuses, or one day it'll happen to you too. He thinks people should <u>stand up</u> against violence and injustice.

Think About Your Feelings and Attitudes to the Poem

1) Pick two words or phrases that <u>stand out to you</u>. If none do, just pick two <u>unusual words or phrases</u>.
2) Write these two words or phrases down. Then write about how they <u>make you feel</u>. If they don't make you feel anything, don't worry — just <u>make something up</u>, as long as it's <u>not too stupid</u>.

> **EXAMPLE** The repeated phrase "my savouring mouth" makes me feel angry with the speaker, as he seems greedy and selfish. He turns a blind eye, and seems more interested in eating than in defending his friends.

Think about the poet's reasons for writing the poem

"Not my Business" isn't just a violent story — it's a <u>rallying call</u> to people living under brutal regimes to stop ignoring the situation and <u>stand up for themselves</u>. In your exam, you could write about how <u>effective</u> you think the poem is in doing this, and why.

Grace Nichols

Grace Nichols was born in Guyana in 1950.
She now lives and writes in Sussex.

© Sheila Geraghty

Suggests she's been feeling like an outsider in England.

Hurricane Hits England

It took a hurricane, to bring her closer
To the landscape.
Half the night she lay awake,
The howling ship of the wind,
5   Its gathering rage,
Like some dark ancestral spectre.
Fearful and reassuring.

Talk to me Huracan
Talk to me Oya
10   Talk to me Shango
And Hattie,
My sweeping, back-home cousin.

Tell me why you visit
An English coast?
15   What is the meaning
Of old tongues
Reaping havoc
In new places?

The blinding illumination,
20   Even as you short-
Circuit us
Into further darkness?

What is the meaning of trees
Falling heavy as whales
25   Their crusted roots
Their cratered graves?

O why is my heart unchained?

Tropical Oya of the Weather,
I am aligning myself to you,
30   I am following the movement of your winds,
I am riding the mystery of your storm.

Ah, sweet mystery,
Come to break the frozen lake in me,
Shaking the foundations of the very trees within me,
35   Come to let me know
That the earth is the earth is the earth.

The voice in the first verse isn't the woman's — it's an observer.

The personification of the storm here hints at the stuff about the storm gods in the rest of the poem.

'Ancestral spectre' means the ghost of a family member from long ago. This introduces the ancient, historical theme.

Caribbean weather is like a family member. It's comforting to her.

'Reaping havoc' means causing chaos.

The lightning strike could be a metaphor for the sudden way she realises that she can be at home anywhere.

Flashes of lightning that caused power cuts.

Shows the power of the storm, and links it with the sea.

She wants to become one with nature.

Her cultural roots have also been revealed by the storm.

Her house feels like a ship in a storm.

She addresses these storm gods and goddesses in a bold, dramatic way.

The name of a Caribbean hurricane in 1961 — a memory from her childhood.

Ancient, religious tone.

Just the sight of the storm is awe-inspiring.

She's really trying to learn something from what's happening.

She feels that the storm has set her free.

All places on Earth are connected — she no longer feels apart from her homeland.

Hurricane Hits England

In 1987, southern England was hit by a <u>massive storm</u> that caused loads of damage. This makes the poet think of the hurricanes that regularly happen in the <u>Caribbean</u>, and she feels <u>spiritually connected</u> to both the Caribbean and England as a result. Which is nice.

You've Got To Know What Happens in the Poem

<u>Lines 1-7</u> A woman is described lying in bed listening to the <u>raging storm</u>. She finds it both <u>scary and comforting</u> at the same time (line 7).

<u>Lines 8-26</u> She asks the <u>storm gods and goddesses</u> why they're visiting England when they usually stick to the Caribbean. She asks why they've uprooted so many massive old <u>trees</u>.

<u>Lines 27-36</u> She <u>joins together</u> with the gods and feels herself <u>riding along</u> with them. She feels <u>set free</u> by the experience, and she's <u>less homesick</u> afterwards.

Learn About the Three Types of Language

1) <u>MYTHICAL LANGUAGE</u> — the poet uses beliefs from the Yorubans in <u>Africa</u> about the weather being <u>controlled by gods</u>. Although these gods are scary, she sees them as positive and <u>well-meaning</u>, and she talks to them in old-fashioned, <u>dramatic language</u>, e.g. lines 29-31.

2) <u>POWERFUL LANGUAGE</u> — there are lots of metaphors and similes (see glossary, p.56-57) to show how <u>devastating</u> the effects of the storm are, e.g. line 24, where the <u>trees</u> are compared to <u>beached whales</u>.

3) <u>PHILOSOPHICAL LANGUAGE</u> — at the start she feels like she's <u>a long way from home</u>. But the hurricane makes her think about whether where she lives is <u>actually important</u> or not (line 36).

Remember the Feelings and Attitudes in the Poem

1) At first she's <u>scared</u> by the storm (lines 5-7).

2) Then she makes the connection with the gods, and seems <u>angry</u> with them for coming to England (lines 13-18).

3) But then she feels a <u>connection</u> with the storm, and finds <u>meaning</u> in it — she sees it as a <u>link with nature</u> and with the Caribbean.

4) She's <u>grateful</u> to the storm — she thinks it's come to help her (line 33).

Think About Your Feelings and Attitudes to the Poem

1) I bet you think I'm going to tell you to pick two words or phrases that <u>stand out to you</u>, don't you?

2) And then to write them down and say how they <u>make you feel</u> and everything. Well I'm not. You should <u>know all that</u> by now. Although technically, I suppose, I just have. Darn.

> **EXAMPLE** When the poet refers to the storm as "some dark ancestral spectre", it makes me feel that there's something mysterious about it. This is more than just a spell of extreme weather — it is something meaningful.

It's another one about culture and identity

Now this is what I call a poem — loads of <u>dramatic</u> talk about lightning and storm gods, and plenty of cracking <u>metaphors</u> to get stuck into. Top stuff. Just remember it's about more than just storms — it shares the <u>cultural theme</u> with several other poems, and that's what Section Two's about...

Identity

Identity in these poems is about <u>who we are</u> and what has made us like this.

> 1) It's about being young or old, male or female, rich or poor, strong or weak, white or black, victim or bully, religious or not.
>
> 2) It's also about <u>where you come from</u>. Which country, region, family background and political system you're from.
>
> 3) Other aspects also make up your identity — your <u>language</u>, your <u>family</u>, your <u>customs</u>, your <u>religion</u>, your <u>history</u> and <u>past experiences</u>. They all make up who you are.

Identity is What we Think of Ourselves

Search for My Tongue (Pages 18-19)

1) The poet speaks two languages, but the English, "foreign", tongue is <u>taking over</u>.
2) She's worried that she has <u>lost her mother tongue</u>, which she feels is part of her <u>identity</u>.
3) She's <u>relieved</u> when she realises that her mother tongue, Gujarati, is strong and will <u>always be there</u>.

Hurricane Hits England (Pages 32-33)

1) The storm <u>frightens the poet</u>, and makes her think about her cultural roots.
2) She has settled in England but does not feel completely <u>at home</u>.
3) The <u>violence of the storm</u> reminds her of her home in the Caribbean, and traditional African beliefs.
4) She regains her sense of identity, and makes <u>connections</u> between England and her homeland. She realises that the Earth is a <u>whole</u>, and that we should never feel cut off from our roots.

Presents from my Aunts in Pakistan (Pages 28-29)

1) The teenager is <u>confused</u> about her identity as she is split between being Pakistani and being English.
2) All the exotic clothes sent by her aunts <u>attract</u> her, but they also <u>embarrass</u> her.
3) She can't work out <u>where she belongs</u>.

Identity is What Others Think of Us

Nothing's Changed (Pages 4-5)

1) This poem traces the anger of a <u>South African</u> man when he returns to the area he used to live in.
2) Although apartheid has been abolished, there is still effectively racial segregation in the area.
3) So the <u>identity</u> of the poem's narrator is affected by what <u>other people</u> in society think.

Unrelated Incidents (Pages 20-21)

1) The poet is angry that his Glaswegian dialect is not taken seriously or <u>trusted in society</u>.
2) The poem shows us that we'd be <u>shocked to hear the news</u> read in this way — because we're used to it being read in a <u>posh accent</u>.
3) So the poem shows us that <u>dialect</u> can be part of identity, because society sometimes <u>judges</u> people by the way they <u>speak</u>.

The poet's sense of identity puts the poem in context

'Limbo' (2-3), 'Love After Love' (24-25), and 'This Room' (26-27) also talk about <u>identity</u>. In some poems, like 'Presents from my Aunts...', it's the poet's <u>main reason</u> for writing. It's important to understand the poet's sense of identity, as it can explain <u>why they feel</u> like they do.

Politics

Politics means how a country is run, and how a <u>government</u> treats its citizens.
Politics affects both <u>society</u> as a whole and <u>individual</u> people.

> 1) Politics can be about the <u>differences</u> between <u>rich and poor</u>.
> 2) It can be about how <u>leaders</u> use and abuse their power.
> 3) Politics can be about certain groups <u>controlling</u> others.

Politics is about Inequality

Nothing's Changed (Pages 4-5)

1) It's set in <u>Nelson Mandela's</u> new South African <u>democracy</u> — apartheid has been officially abolished.
2) But the poem's narrator finds that <u>there are still inequalities</u> — the "whites only inn" makes him feel unwelcome because of his colour, so he has to go to the grimy "working man's cafe".
3) So the political angle here is all about <u>racial inequality</u>.

Two Scavengers in a Truck... (Pages 10-11)

1) The <u>gap</u> between the <u>rich and poor</u> is very clear.
2) The USA prides itself on <u>equal opportunity</u> for all — but here we're shown the "<u>gulf</u>" that exists between the "casually coifed" young woman and the "grungy" garbagemen.
3) The poet thinks this situation is wrong and <u>unfair</u>.

"If I ever get my hands on that barber..."

Vultures (Pages 14-15)

1) The Commandant represents <u>Nazi Germany's abuse of power</u> — the Nazis <u>murdered</u> millions of Jews because they believed they were inferior.
2) This <u>destruction of another culture</u> and race was government policy.

It's about People's Attitudes and Opinions

What Were They Like? (Pages 16-17)

1) Many people were <u>against</u> America's involvement in the <u>Vietnam War</u> in the 1960s and 1970s.
2) The poet shows her <u>opposition to the war</u> by showing the <u>damage</u> done to the Vietnamese people and culture.

Unrelated Incidents (Pages 20-21)

1) 'Unrelated Incidents' is about the power that <u>language</u> holds. The poet says a Glaswegian accent delivering the news would not be believed or respected.
2) The political dimension here involves us all and the <u>judgements</u> we make about people because of <u>how they speak</u>. The poet shows that people see some accents as <u>better</u> than others.

You don't have to be Jeremy Paxman

Don't panic if your knowledge of world politics is a bit <u>sketchy</u>. It can help to know the odd fact, but you can work a lot out <u>just from the poems</u> — so don't go thinking you have to know the complete socio-political history of Nigeria. It's an English exam, not Politics.

Change

Some of the poems deal with a <u>change</u> in the poet's life, or in the world. This can be a change of <u>circumstance</u> or a change in <u>personality</u>, and it can be <u>positive</u> or <u>negative</u>.

1) People can experience a change which <u>frees them</u> from their problems.
2) Things can change for the <u>worse</u> — on a temporary or permanent basis.
3) Things may <u>appear</u> to have changed but in fact be very <u>similar</u> to how they always were.

Things can Change for the Better

Search For My Tongue (Pages 18-19)

1) The poet is worried that she's <u>lost her mother tongue</u> (Gujarati) because her "foreign" tongue (English) has taken over.
2) A <u>positive change</u> occurs when she dreams in Gujarati and realises it will <u>always be with her</u>.
3) This change is <u>internal</u> and <u>personal</u>.

Found it

This Room (Pages 26-27)

1) This poem is about a <u>sudden and unexpected change</u> in the poet's life.
2) We <u>don't know exactly</u> what this change is.
3) But it's clearly a <u>positive</u> one, that will affect her life in a <u>massive</u> way — "This is the time and place / to be alive".

Change can be a Bad Thing

Nothing's Changed (Pages 4-5)

1) In between the poet's last visit to District Six and the visit he describes in the poem, there's been a major <u>political change</u> — apartheid has been abolished.
2) In theory, this is a <u>positive</u> change, people of different races are now <u>officially equal</u>.
3) But, in terms of <u>attitudes</u> and the <u>way people live</u>, the poet says that things <u>haven't changed</u> at all — black people are still treated as inferior.

What Were They Like? (Pages 16-17)

1) The poet describes a <u>negative change</u> — the traditional Vietnamese culture has been <u>destroyed</u>.
2) It seems like this is a <u>permanent loss</u>. The poem concludes with, "It is silent now".

Presents from my Aunts in Pakistan (Pages 28-29)

1) In this poem, the poet is <u>afraid of change</u> — she feels "alien in the sitting-room" when she tries on the Pakistani clothes, because she's not used to wearing them.
2) This causes her way of <u>thinking about herself</u> to change. She now has to work out whether she's <u>English or Pakistani</u>, or <u>both</u>, whereas before she'd thought of herself just as English.
3) She also mentions a <u>change in the past</u>, i.e. when she first came to England from Pakistan as a small child.

Some poets call for change, others criticise it

It's a fairly open topic, so there are loads of <u>angles</u> you could tackle it from. The changes described in any two of the poems on this page will have things <u>in common</u> and things that are <u>different</u>.

People

The poems talk about the lives of both <u>individuals</u> and <u>groups</u> of people.

> 1) Some poets are interested in <u>society</u>, and people's attitudes towards, and treatment of, each other.
> 2) Sometimes one <u>group</u> of people live a completely <u>different lifestyle</u> to that of another group.
> 3) Other poets write about individual people, and their unique and personal feelings and experiences.

People are Affected by Society

Half-Caste (Pages 22-23)

1) The <u>words</u> people use can show the <u>attitudes</u> they have towards different groups in society.
2) The poet says the term "half-caste" is a <u>silly</u> and <u>offensive</u> way of describing mixed-race people.
3) He <u>challenges</u> people to <u>think again</u> about how they see each other.

Not my Business (Pages 30-31)

1) The poet shows how <u>terrible</u> it is to be ruled by a <u>violent regime</u>.
2) He says that if people <u>ignore</u> what's happening to their neighbours, things will get worse and eventually <u>everyone</u> will suffer.
3) He encourages people to <u>stand up</u> for each other, in order to create a <u>better society</u>.

Two Scavengers in a Truck... (Pages 10-11)

1) There's a clear <u>division</u> between the two pairs of people in the poem.
2) The scavengers can only <u>stare</u> at the couple in the Merc and <u>imagine</u> what it would be like to live like them — they can never cross the "small gulf" between them.
3) The poet <u>criticises American society</u> for not doing anything about this <u>social divide</u>. His reference to "democracy" is <u>sarcastic</u> — democracy suggests <u>equality</u>, but the two sets of people in the poem are not treated equally by society at all.

Some People are On Their Own

Island Man (Pages 6-7)

1) This poem is about an <u>individual</u> who feels on his own.
2) The man in 'Island Man' has a clear sense of <u>where he belongs</u>, i.e. in the Caribbean, not in London.
3) It's a fairly straightforward and familiar story of being <u>homesick</u>.

Hurricane Hits England (Pages 32-33)

1) Although <u>millions</u> of people were affected by the 1987 storm, the poet in 'Hurricane Hits England' talks about her own <u>personal experience</u> of it.
2) The storm triggers a <u>moment of realisation</u> that changes the way she approaches life.
3) The storm makes her see that it <u>doesn't make sense</u> to feel homesick, because all parts of the Earth are <u>connected</u> to each other.

We are all individuals (apart from me)

'Presents from my Aunts...' (28-29), 'Night of the Scorpion' (12-13) and 'Vultures' (14-15) are also good poems for this topic. All the people in these poems encounter <u>problems</u> of some sort — you could compare someone who <u>solves their problems</u> with someone who <u>can't</u>, and discuss why.

First Person

If a poet writes in the <u>first person</u>, they use words like "<u>I</u>" and "<u>me</u>", rather than "she" or "him".

> 1) Writing in the first person allows the poet to <u>use their voice directly</u>.
> 2) This allows them to say <u>how they feel</u> and <u>what they mean</u>.
> 3) The first person lets us see things from the poet or character's <u>point of view</u>.

Some Poets "Look Inside Themselves"

Presents from my Aunts in Pakistan (Pages 28-29)

1) The first person point of view in this poem lets us see how <u>confused</u> and <u>uncertain</u> the girl is.
2) Phrases like "I could never be as lovely / as those clothes" (lines 18-19) help us to understand her <u>emotions</u> in a way that wouldn't be possible without the first person style.

Search For My Tongue (Pages 18-19)

1) The poet uses a <u>conversational</u> tone ("You ask me what I mean"), so that it sounds like she's explaining her thoughts to you, as if you're a <u>friend</u>.
2) Her descriptions of her <u>dreams</u> give us an idea of how her mind works.
3) This is important to the idea that her mother tongue is <u>living inside her</u>.

"You can't have mine"

This Room (Pages 26-27)

1) The poem's about a very <u>personal</u> experience.
2) The poet uses the first person voice to show us how <u>important</u> the event is to her.
3) <u>Strange images</u> like her hands being "outside, clapping" show the weird <u>feelings</u> she's experiencing.

Some Poets Want to Inform or Persuade People

Nothing's Changed (Pages 4-5)

1) The poet's voice allows us to experience the <u>inequality</u> through <u>his eyes</u>.
2) He sees the <u>luxury</u> of the white people's inn — "I press my nose / to the clear panes" (lines 27-28) — but knows he's not welcome there.
3) Using the first person allows his message to be direct — he wants us to realise how <u>unfair</u> it is.

Not my Business (Pages 30-31)

1) We hear the voice of an onlooker who <u>doesn't get involved</u> when people are abused.
2) He shows the <u>selfishness</u> of this attitude — "What business of mine is it...?"
3) The poet <u>disagrees</u> with this attitude — he wants people to <u>stand up for each other</u>.

Night of the Scorpion (Pages 12-13)

1) We see events unfold through the eyes of a <u>child</u> — "I watched the holy man perform his rites" (line 42).
2) He's <u>scared</u> and <u>confused</u> by the religious response to his mother being stung by the scorpion.
3) Using the first person shows us how <u>odd</u> the religious people's actions seem to the boy.

The first person lets the poet speak directly to the reader

'Limbo' (pages 2-3) 'Half-Caste' (pages 22-23) and 'Hurricane...' (32-33) also use the first person. It makes a massive difference to the <u>effect</u> of the poem, as it lets the poet talk <u>personally</u> — poems like 'Not my Business' would really <u>lose their impact</u> if it was just "he" or "she" instead of "I".

Specific Cultural References

Cultural references include beliefs, customs, religions, history, literature and loads of other things. They make up a community's <u>way of life</u>.

> 1) There can be <u>different cultures</u> within the <u>same society</u>.
> 2) Some people can grow up <u>surrounded</u> by a particular culture <u>without</u> really feeling <u>part of it</u>.
> 3) Some cultures <u>classify</u> people according to things like <u>race</u>, <u>gender</u> and <u>wealth</u>, rather than believing that everyone is equal.

Some Cultures are Divided

Two Scavengers in a Truck... (Pages 10-11)

1) The <u>language</u> of the poem, e.g. "downtown" and "garbage truck", sounds <u>typically American</u>.
2) The culture of the USA claims to value <u>equal opportunity</u> and <u>democracy</u>.
3) But it seems like the binmen will <u>never be able</u> to live like the rich couple.
4) So the idea that "everything is always possible" in America (line 30), is shown to be <u>false</u>.

This culture isn't featured

Nothing's Changed (Pages 4-5)

1) The culture here is the divided society of modern <u>South Africa</u>. The poet mentions that it's District Six because this is the area he knows, but it applies to the <u>whole country</u>.
2) Now that apartheid has ended, people of <u>different races</u> should be living as <u>equals</u> — but in fact, the <u>segregation still exists</u>, even under Mandela's government.
3) There's the odd use of South African <u>slang</u>, such as "boy" and "bunny chows", which adds to the feel of the poem being set in <u>South Africa</u>.

Limbo (Pages 2-3)

1) The theme here is <u>slavery</u>. Although it was abolished in the 19th Century, the <u>history</u> of slavery is still <u>important</u> to many black people today.
2) There are references to life as a slave, such as the <u>cramped conditions</u> on the slave ships.
3) The <u>limbo dance</u> is strongly linked to this West Indian slave culture.

People can Become Separated from their Culture

Night of the Scorpion (Pages 12-13)

1) It's set in a <u>Hindu</u> community in India.
2) The locals believe in <u>reincarnation</u>. The prayers relate to <u>purifying the soul</u> for the next life.
3) But the boy's father is a "sceptic", so the boy's probably grown up in a <u>non-Hindu</u> household — which must make the Hindu ceremony seem very <u>odd</u>.

Hurricane Hits England (Pages 32-33)

1) Before the storm, the poet has been feeling like an <u>outsider</u> to English culture.
2) She refers to African <u>storm gods and goddesses</u> — Huracan, Oya and Shango.
3) The poet uses these as a link to her <u>Caribbean roots</u> — black Caribbeans were originally from Africa.

Culture can be the central theme or provide the setting

'What Were They Like?' (pages 16-17), 'Search For My Tongue' (18-19), 'Not my Business' (30-31), and 'Presents from My Aunts...' (28-29) also fit into this topic. There are loads of <u>different cultures</u> in the anthology, which means there's plenty of <u>variety</u> to keep you <u>on your toes</u>.

Description

Poets use various ways of <u>describing</u> things to keep the reader <u>interested</u>.

> 1) Poets can use exciting or unexpected <u>adjectives</u> to describe things or people.
>
> 2) They can use <u>comparisons</u>, strong <u>opinions</u> or <u>humour</u> if they want to give a particular <u>impression</u> of something or someone.
>
> 3) Contrasting descriptions can be used to show <u>differences</u> between people or places.

> An adjective is a word that <u>describes</u> something, e.g. the <u>hungry</u> cat.

Poets Describe People

Two Scavengers in a Truck... (Pages 10-11)

1) There's a sharp <u>contrast</u> between the <u>appearances</u> of the "grungy" binmen and the "elegant couple".
2) There's also a <u>suggested</u> contrast between <u>how hard</u> the two pairs of people <u>work</u> — the "scavengers" have been "up since four a.m.", while the driver of the Mercedes is still "on the way" to the office.

Presents from my Aunts in Pakistan (Pages 28-29)

1) The poet's descriptions of the <u>presents</u> show her mixed feelings.
2) They're "<u>lovely</u>" but also "<u>broad and stiff</u>", showing they're <u>uncomfortable</u>.
3) The simile "glistening like an orange" (line 4) shows they seem <u>exotic</u> to her, rather than normal.

Blessing (Pages 8-9)

1) The descriptions of the <u>rush for water</u> from the burst pipe show how <u>desperate</u> the people are.
2) They have "frantic hands", which shows the <u>urgency</u> with which they collect the water.
3) <u>Basic items</u> like "tin mugs" and "plastic buckets" seem to be the only possessions the people own, which emphasises how <u>poor</u> they are.

Poets Describe Places

Nothing's Changed (Pages 4-5)

1) The poet's descriptions of "hard stones", "seeding grasses" and "amiable weeds" in the first verse show that District Six is <u>neglected</u> and <u>run-down</u>.
2) The <u>differences</u> between the lives of whites and non-whites are shown by the contrast between the "<u>haute cuisine</u>" at the "up-market" inn and the "<u>bunny chows</u>" eaten at "a plastic table's top" at the cafe.

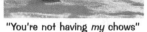
"You're not having *my* chows"

Island Man (Pages 6-7)

1) The "emerald island" in the Caribbean, with its "wild seabirds", sounds like an <u>unspoilt paradise</u>.
2) By contrast, the "grey metallic soar" of London traffic sounds <u>dreary and unnatural</u>.
3) We only hear the <u>good things about the Caribbean</u> and the <u>bad things about London</u>, which makes us realise he's longing to be back home.

Compare the different descriptions in a poem

Poets use descriptions to make their poems more interesting to read. Sometimes poets can use a lot of descriptions which <u>add together</u> to create an <u>overall picture</u> of something. But also look out for descriptions which <u>contrast</u> with something else in another part of the poem.

Metaphor

A <u>metaphor</u> is when something is described as if it's <u>something else</u> for effect.

> 1) Metaphors can be used to <u>emphasise</u> just how big, fast, fat, brilliant, rubbish or weird something or someone is.
>
> 2) An <u>extended</u> metaphor (also called a <u>running</u> metaphor) is when a writer uses a metaphor again and again, developing it to show <u>more</u> about the thing being described.

Don't confuse metaphors with similes. A <u>simile</u> says something is <u>like</u> something else — a <u>metaphor</u> says it actually <u>is</u> something else.

Metaphors can Describe People's Lives

Vultures (Pages 14-15)

1) The vultures are ugly and <u>disgusting</u>, with "a dump of gross / feathers", but are capable of <u>gentleness</u>.
2) This leads to the description of the Commandant, who <u>murders</u> people every day yet <u>loves his child</u>.
3) So the <u>vultures</u> are a metaphor for the Commandant — although we <u>don't realise</u> this at first, as more than half the poem has passed before the Commandant is mentioned.

Blessing (Pages 8-9)

1) Water is described as "fortune" and "silver", showing how <u>valuable</u> it is to the people of the slum.
2) The people become a "congregation", creating a <u>religious</u> feel — they're <u>worshipping</u> this gift from "a kindly god".
3) The metaphor "the blessing sings / over their small bones" (lines 22 and 23), shows that the burst water pipe is like an <u>answer to the children's prayers</u>.

Metaphors can Describe Feelings

This Room (Pages 26-27)

1) The <u>room</u> and the <u>furniture</u> become <u>alive</u>. This shows how the poet feels suddenly <u>free</u> after the special event that's happened.
2) The fact that such <u>ordinary</u> objects are "rising up to crash through clouds" (line 9) shows how <u>extraordinary</u> the situation is.
3) At the end of the poem, individual <u>parts of the poet's body</u> become separate from each other — showing how <u>confused</u> she is by all the excitement.

Any second...NOW

Search For My Tongue (Pages 18-19)

1) The poet's <u>mother tongue</u> (Gujarati) is described as a <u>living thing</u> — she's worried that it will "rot and die".
2) This idea becomes an <u>extended metaphor</u>. Gujarati is described metaphorically as a <u>flower</u>, and words like "bud" and "blossoms" show that it's <u>growing back</u>.
3) This suggests that her mother tongue is <u>rooted</u> in her.

Half-Caste (Pages 22-23)

1) The poet <u>mocks</u> the term "half-caste" by comparing mixed-race people to classical music and paintings — the idea of calling these things "half" just because they're mixed seems <u>silly</u>.
2) He then uses the "half" idea to describe <u>body parts</u>, e.g. "I offer yu half-a-hand". This could be seen as a <u>metaphor</u> for the poet being <u>unwelcoming</u> to racists.
3) He mixes in <u>humour</u> with his metaphors, so that his point about the <u>stupidity</u> of the word is clear.

Metaphors make poems more interesting

Remember to say <u>why</u> you think a poet has chosen to use a particular metaphor. Think about what <u>impression</u> the metaphor gives. If you can work this out, it's a big clue to the poet's <u>message</u>.

Unusual Presentation

A lot of these poems have an <u>odd layout</u>. This might look daft at first, but it can be effective.

> 1) The way a poem looks on the page affects your <u>first impressions</u> of it.
> 2) <u>Regular</u> styles of presentation help to <u>maintain</u> an effect throughout the <u>whole poem</u>.
> 3) <u>Irregular</u> layout can create different effects in different parts of the poem.
>   It can also help the poet to create a sense of disorder or conflict.

Presentation can Create an Overall Effect...

What Were They Like? (Pages 16-17)

1) The questions and answers are <u>numbered</u> so that it looks like a "real" enquiry.
2) Each question can be <u>matched</u> to its corresponding answer.
3) Each pair covers a <u>particular aspect</u> of the Vietnamese culture.
4) The <u>failure</u> to come up with any satisfactory answers is part of the poet's criticism of the war.

Unrelated Incidents (Pages 20-21)

1) The <u>short lines</u> of almost even length make the poem look like a newsreader's <u>autocue</u>.
2) This adds <u>humour</u> to the poem, and reinforces the poem's theme.
3) The short lines also make the poem sound <u>hard-hitting</u> and <u>to-the-point</u>.

...Or various Different Effects within the poem

Limbo (Pages 2-3)

1) The <u>line lengths</u> vary a lot — some of the lines are quite long, while others are only one word.
2) The <u>longer</u> lines, e.g. line 7, create an impression of the <u>ongoing cruelty</u> of slave conditions.
3) Shorter lines describe movement, e.g. the <u>repetition</u> of "down" makes it feel like an <u>ongoing</u> descent.
4) The repeated "*limbo like me*" lines <u>connect</u> the poet to <u>slave culture</u> and <u>history</u>.

Search For My Tongue (Pages 18-19)

1) Seeing the <u>Gujarati script</u> allows us to see how <u>different</u> it is to English.
2) This gives us an insight into <u>why</u> it's so <u>important</u> to the poet — it represents a <u>different side</u> of her personality.
3) The Gujarati words are spelled out phonetically (see glossary p.57) in English too, so we can hear what they <u>sound like</u>.

Presentation can reflect the poem's theme

'Two Scavengers in a Truck, Two Beautiful People in a Mercedes' (pages 10-11), and 'Presents from my Aunts in Pakistan' (28-29) also have unusual presentation. It's all about creating a <u>visual effect</u>, to add to the effect of the words and <u>illustrate</u> whatever point the poet is making.

Non-Standard English

Standard English means talking in a posh accent, using "correct" grammar and no slang.
So non-standard English means anything else.

1) Non-standard English can mean talking in a regional accent, like Scouse or Geordie.
2) It includes using different forms of grammar, like West Indian creole.
3) All slang words are non-standard English.
4) Non-standard English can mean being creative with the words you use.

Language Links a Poem with its Background

Limbo (Pages 2-3)

1) The poet uses the West Indian creole dialect that slaves often spoke in.
2) This links the poem with slave history, and allows the poet to write from a slave's point-of-view.
3) The simplified grammar of creole gives the poem a harsh sound, e.g. "stick hit sound" —
   this adds to the impression of the cruelty of slave punishment.

Island Man (Pages 6-7)

1) In this poem, individual words are used in unusual ways, making us see several meanings.
2) "Wombing" is used to describe the gentle, comforting sounds of the sea, but it also
   connects the sea to the man's birth, showing it's where he belongs.
3) Some words could apply to aspects of life in both the Caribbean and London,
   e.g. "roar" is used to describe the London traffic, but it also sounds like the sea.

Dialect can be In-Yer-Face

Unrelated Incidents (Pages 20-21)

1) The whole poem is written phonetically to represent a Glaswegian accent.
2) This emphasises how different it sounds to standard English.
3) The poet shows he's not ashamed to speak in his natural voice — he wants it
   to be heard, because he thinks we hear enough posh accents in public life.

Half-Caste (Pages 22-23)

1) The West Indian dialect sounds more direct than standard English,
   so the poet can challenge the reader, e.g. "wha yu mean".
2) Non-standard English allows the reader to "hear" the
   poet's voice, so it feels more like a conversation.
3) The mixture of standard and non-standard English reflects the
   poet's mixed background, and shows that he's proud of it.

De language adds to de effeck

With poems like 'Half-Caste', it's easy to think the poet's just showing off by writing in dialect.
But the poems really wouldn't be very effective if they just said, "In my opinion, it's perfectly
acceptable to speak in dialect," or something like that. The sound of the poem when spoken is vital.

Particular Places

The descriptions of <u>places</u> are strongly linked to the <u>message</u> of some of these poems.

> 1) Some poets describe their <u>homes</u> or <u>birthplaces</u>.
> 2) Other poets use a setting as a background for the <u>topic</u> they want to talk about.
> 3) Places aren't always described in detail — sometimes a <u>lack of detail</u> can be effective.

Places can be Connected to Identity

Presents from my Aunts in Pakistan (Pages 28-29)

1) The poet only <u>vaguely</u> remembers Pakistan — she relies on <u>photos</u> and <u>newspapers</u> to describe it.
2) Pakistan is described as "fractured", showing the poet's <u>split identity</u>.
3) The poet's <u>imaginings</u> of Pakistan are of <u>mysterious</u> "shaded rooms" and beggars.
4) These aren't very positive thoughts — she's <u>uncomfortable</u> with the idea of being Pakistani.

Hurricane Hits England (Pages 32-33)

1) The woman wants to feel "closer / To the landscape" (lines 1-2) — she feels <u>emotional</u> about places.
2) At the start of the poem, she feels a <u>long way</u> from her home in the Caribbean.
3) When England gets a taste of a Caribbean-style storm, it makes her realise that <u>everywhere on Earth is connected</u> — so places aren't that important after all.

Places can Stand for the State of Society

Two Scavengers in a Truck... (Pages 10-11)

1) It's San Francisco, though it could be <u>many places in America</u>.
2) The description of the setting in lines 1-2 sounds <u>unremarkable</u>, suggesting the situation the poet describes is not unusual — this is normal, <u>everyday life</u>.
3) The situation represents the poet's views on <u>America</u> in general, and the unfair <u>division</u> between rich and poor.

Nothing's Changed (Pages 4-5)

1) Harsh-sounding descriptions of stones and litter <u>set the tone</u> for the <u>bitterness</u> of the poem.
2) The poet instinctively <u>recognises</u> his home district — "my feet know, / and my hands".
3) There's a clear <u>division</u> in one street — the plush inn at one end, and the grimy cafe, "down the road". This shows how the blacks and whites live <u>very close</u> to each other, but live <u>separate</u> lives.

Vultures (Pages 14-15)

1) Bleak descriptions of the <u>vultures' habitat</u> create a <u>dark, miserable mood</u>.
2) The poem starts at dawn, but there's only "greyness" and "drizzle" — there's <u>no sign of the sun</u>.
3) There's <u>no other life</u> in this place — just a "dead tree", introducing the theme of <u>death</u>.
4) The <u>dark atmosphere</u> of this place sets the tone for the <u>evil deeds</u> of the vultures and the Commandant.

Find out some bits and pieces about the setting

Often the setting is just a <u>backdrop</u> to the poem's issues. But in some poems, like 'Hurricane Hits England', it's the <u>main theme</u>, so it's useful to know a thing or two about these places.

Two Cultures

Some of the poets talk about the effects of having <u>two different cultures</u> in their lives.

> 1) Having a <u>mixed background</u> can make people feel like they're <u>torn</u> between two cultures.
>
> 2) Sometimes people have <u>moved</u> to a different country and <u>miss</u> the culture they're <u>used to</u>.
>
> 3) Some cultures are <u>divided</u>, with one group of people trying to control another.

Some Cultures Clash

Search For My Tongue (Pages 18-19)

1) The poet sees the English and Asian cultures as being <u>separate parts of her</u>, that <u>can't</u> be brought together.

2) This <u>opposition</u> is shown through <u>languages</u> — her mother tongue (Gujarati) "could not really know the other" (English).

3) By the end of the poem, the two languages seem to be <u>fighting each other</u> — Gujarati "ties the other tongue in knots" (line 33).

Unrelated Incidents (Pages 20-21)

1) The two cultures in this poem are <u>posh English</u> culture and <u>working-class Scottish</u> culture.

2) Again, the division is shown through <u>language</u> — standard BBC English versus regional accents. The poet believes that people see <u>regional accents</u> as <u>inferior</u>.

3) The poet <u>stands up</u> for his own background, by showing he's <u>not ashamed</u> of the way he talks.

Presents from my Aunts in Pakistan (Pages 28-29)

1) The poet has spent most of her life in <u>England</u>, so the presents from <u>Pakistan</u> seem <u>foreign</u> to her, even though she was born in Pakistan and has relatives there.

2) The poet feels that the two cultures <u>don't mix well</u> — Pakistani clothes make her feel "alien".

3) The fact that she belongs to two cultures seems to <u>confuse</u> her rather than help her — at the end she seems to feel like an <u>outsider to both</u>.

Cultures can Mix Together

Half-Caste (Pages 22-23)

1) The poet in 'Half-Caste' reckons cultures <u>can mix together</u>.

2) The theme is that it's <u>good</u> when <u>cultures mix</u> — he compares it to "when light an shadow / mix in de sky" (line 14), suggesting it's <u>natural</u>.

3) The poet seems <u>proud</u> of his own <u>mixed background</u>.

Hurricane Hits England (Pages 32-33)

1) The woman in the poem <u>doesn't feel a part</u> of English culture — she misses the Caribbean.

2) At the start of the poem, the cultures seem very <u>different</u>, and she feels a <u>long way from home</u>.

3) By the end, thanks to the storm gods, the poet sees all places and cultures as <u>being connected</u>, and suggests the differences <u>aren't important</u> after all — "the earth is the earth is the earth" (line 36).

Belonging to two cultures can be good or bad

The main difference between the ways the poets talk about having two cultures in their lives is that some <u>like it</u> and some <u>don't</u>. Remember that everyone's background is <u>different</u>, so it's <u>not</u> as simple as some of them moaning about it and some of them making the most of it.

Universal Ideas

If something's universal, it could apply to any place or time, rather than just being about the exact situation in the poem. Many of these poets deal with universal themes.

1) Ideas like loneliness, equality and identity have interested people all over the world for ages.

2) Some poets talk about a specific situation as a way of making a point about people or society in general.

Some Poets Talk About Equality

Half-Caste (Pages 22-23)

1) This poem deals with ideas of inferiority and equality.
2) The poet thinks the expression "half-caste" suggests mixed-race people are inferior.
3) He challenges this viewpoint, sarcastically saying that he casts "half-a-shadow".
4) He turns the idea around by saying that it's the people who use the term "half-caste" who are incomplete because they don't use "de whole of yu mind".

Two Scavengers in a Truck... (Pages 10-11)

1) The theme of this poem is how people allow inequality to happen.
2) We see how the garbagemen are fascinated with the rich people, but the rich couple aren't interested in the garbagemen.
3) This suggests that people are selfish, and ignore inequalities — as long as they benefit from them.

Poems can be About Aspects of Humanity

Love After Love (Pages 24-25)

1) This poem is about being alone.
2) The poet challenges the assumption that people are incomplete without another person.
3) The poet basically says you're often better off on your own. He advises the reader to "Give back your heart / To itself," as relationships can make you betray your true identity.

This Room (Pages 26-27)

1) The poem is about a special moment in life, when things suddenly change for the better.
2) We don't find out exactly what this moment is, and that adds to the universal feel of it. It stands for any special, improbable event in someone's life.
3) There's a sense of optimism about the poem — "This is the time and place / to be alive". The message is that you should make the most of opportunities when they come along.

Vultures (Pages 14-15)

1) It's about good and evil. The poet first talks about the vultures and the Commandant, then discusses good and evil in general.
2) Lines 22-29 are universal, and discuss how love and evil can exist separately in the same person.
3) Lines 41-51 are also universal, and sum up the theme of the poem. The poet asks whether we should be grateful that evil people are capable of love, or depressed because that love will always be infected with evil.

Specific examples can stand for things in general

Universal ideas are also dealt with in 'Nothing's Changed' (pages 4-5), 'Not my Business' (pages 30-31) and 'Hurricane Hits England' (32-33). The trick with this theme is to say how specific situations can be applied to life in general.

Traditions

A <u>tradition</u> is a belief or custom that's been <u>passed down</u> from one generation to the next.

> 1) Some poets use traditions as a <u>link</u> to their <u>culture</u>, <u>past</u> or <u>identity</u>.
> 2) Sometimes they <u>criticise</u> traditions, seeing them as just silly <u>superstitions</u>.
> 3) Traditions can seem <u>distant</u> and <u>mysterious</u>.

Some Traditions are Mysterious

Night of the Scorpion (Pages 12-13)

1) The poet describes traditional <u>Hindu</u> beliefs about <u>reincarnation</u>.
2) The villagers believe that the <u>pain</u> the boy's mother is feeling will mean her <u>next life</u> will be <u>better</u>.
3) The poet seems <u>separated</u> from this, probably because his dad isn't a Hindu believer.
   So these traditions appear <u>strange</u> and <u>superstitious</u> to him.
4) The poet's description of them calmly sitting in a <u>circle</u> around his mother, while she "twisted through and through", sounds <u>critical</u> — he wishes they would do something more <u>practical</u> to help her.

What Were They Like? (Pages 16-17)

1) The poem is about <u>Vietnamese</u> traditions and culture, written as though these are lost forever.
2) The descriptions of these traditions are <u>unclear</u>. This emphasises that the war has <u>destroyed</u> this culture and its traditions for ever.
3) There's a <u>mysterious but beautiful</u> feel to this way of life — "stone lanterns illumined pleasant ways" (Answer 1). This adds to the poet's <u>anger</u> at what has happened to Vietnam.
4) But there are also questions about <u>ceremonies</u> and <u>ornaments</u>, showing that they had plenty <u>in common with us</u> too.

Traditions can Provide a Link with the Past

Limbo (Pages 2-3)

1) The <u>limbo dance</u> originated from memories of being transported in cramped <u>slave ships</u>.
2) It's now a traditional <u>West Indian</u> dance that celebrates black people's <u>survival</u> and <u>freedom</u>.
3) The poet uses the "*Limbo like me*" refrain to emphasise his <u>links with black history</u>.
4) His <u>links</u> with the slaves help him to <u>break free</u> at the end of the poem —
   "the drummers are praising me".

"Remind me, why are we doing this?"

Hurricane Hits England (Pages 32-33)

1) Traditional <u>African</u> beliefs say that the weather is caused by <u>gods</u>.
2) The poet calls on the <u>storm gods and goddesses</u> (Huracan, Oya and Shango) to explain <u>why</u> the hurricane has come to England.
3) The poet uses these gods as a <u>link</u> with her <u>Caribbean roots</u>. She feels a new sense of <u>freedom</u> and <u>purpose</u> as a result.

Traditions can be described positively or negatively

Traditions are also explored in 'Presents from my Aunts in Pakistan' (pages 28-29). Most of the poets have pretty strong opinions about tradition and culture — they're generally either <u>well into it</u>, or they think it's <u>a bit silly</u>, even if they don't say so outright.

Sample Essay and Exam Method: Identity

FOLLOW THIS FIVE-STEP METHOD FOR A DECENT ANSWER EVERY TIME

First, the basics. You get <u>45 minutes</u> for this question in the exam. It's <u>crucial</u> that you spend about <u>10 minutes</u> of this <u>planning</u> your answer — if you don't, your essay will be a big pile of pants.

Remember — <u>every question</u> deals with a theme. The theme for this sample question is <u>identity</u>. Other key words in this question are "<u>factors</u>", "<u>poetic devices</u>" and "<u>feelings</u>". Refer to them throughout your essay. I've highlighted them in the sample essay on the next page.

It's essential that you <u>compare</u> the two poems. Good comparing words and phrases are:

• on the other hand	• contrasting with	• more/less	• though
• similarly	• however	• whereas	• likewise

1) Write a Bit About the Theme

1) Give a <u>definition</u> of the theme. You don't have to go into any detail — this example is quite basic.

2) <u>Explain</u> how the theme relates to the poems you will write about.

2) Write About the First Pointer: "the factors that make up identity"

1) You could write about <u>nationality</u>, <u>age</u>, <u>gender</u>, <u>clothes</u>, <u>culture</u>, or anything else that's important to what the poets think about identity. Say how the poet presents these factors, and <u>how</u> they're shown to be <u>important</u> to identity.

2) You've got to <u>compare</u> the two poems — say how they're <u>similar</u> and how they're <u>different</u>.

3) Write About the Second Pointer: "the poetic devices used"

1) <u>Poetic devices</u> means the little <u>tricks</u> the poets use to make their poems more <u>interesting</u>. There are some examples in the box below (look at the glossary, p.56-57, if you're forgotten what any of these mean).

• alliteration	• rhythm	• metaphors	• imagery	• layout
• onomatopoeia	• irony	• similes	• tone	• structure

2) Make sure you say what <u>effect</u> these devices have.

3) It's vital that you <u>compare</u> the devices used in the two poems, and the effects they have.

4) Write About the Third Pointer: "the poets' feelings about identity"

1) Say how the poets' identity affects <u>how they see themselves</u>. If their identity causes them <u>problems</u>, say what kind of problems they are and how the poets try to <u>deal with them</u>.

2) You could talk about whether the poets are comfortable with their identity or not. Say whether they've <u>dealt with their problems</u>, or if they're <u>still unsure</u> about their identity at the end of the poem.

3) Have a look at <u>Section One</u> for some ideas about the poets' feelings.

4) Compare, compare, <u>compare</u>.

There might be more than three bullet points. However many there are, write about <u>all of them</u>.

5) Write About How the Poems Make You Feel

1) Say which poem you <u>preferred</u> and <u>why</u>.

2) Say what you've <u>learnt</u> about the theme.

3) Show some <u>empathy</u> — connect the poem to <u>your own feelings and experiences</u>.

Sample Essay and Exam Method: Identity

THIS SAMPLE ESSAY USES THE FIVE-STEP METHOD

Learn the stuff on your poems and themes, then use this method in the exam, and you'll be fine.

Question 1 Compare the poets' feelings about identity in 'Presents from my Aunts in Pakistan' and one other poem.

Compare:
- the factors that make up identity
- the poetic devices used
- the poets' feelings about identity.

These pointers are here to make your life easier. So it's vital that you cover all of them in your answer.

Identity means how we see ourselves, as individuals or groups of people. In 'Presents from my Aunts in Pakistan' and 'Search For My Tongue', the poets discuss their differing ideas about identity.

Talk about the theme straightaway — that's what the question is about.

In 'Presents from my Aunts in Pakistan', identity is connected to clothes, background and family customs. The teenager in 'Presents...' can't decide which culture she belongs to. The Pakistani clothes sent to her seem very strange and not part of her — she says she "longed / for denim and corduroy". In 'Search for My Tongue', on the other hand, language is the most important factor. The poet in 'Search...' is very concerned that she has "lost the first one, the mother tongue", which is clearly a big part of her identity.

One poetic device that both poets use is unusual layout. The layout of 'Presents...' is very haphazard with lines of different lengths which start all over the page, showing the young girl's confusion. Likewise, 'Search...' has an unusual layout because at the centre of the poem we see the Gujarati writing, with phonetic spelling so we can hear what it sounds like when spoken. It is placed at the centre because it is central to her identity.

Make sure you constantly refer to the key words in the question — I've highlighted them.

There are several other interesting poetic devices in these poems. Both use comparisons to explain their ideas. In 'Search...', the two languages, English and Gujarati, are like plants growing in her mouth and fighting each other. The mother tongue wins in the end: it "grows longer, grows moist, grows strong veins, / it ties the other tongue in knots". Similarly, when the girl in 'Presents...' tries on the Pakistani clothes, she feels "alien in the sitting-room", showing that they make her feel out of place in England.

You have to back up the points you make with quotes.

The girl in 'Presents...' never resolves her identity crisis. She feels that she "could never be as lovely / as those clothes", which shows that she thinks she cannot fit in with this element of her background, no matter how hard she tries. At the end of the poem she says she is "of no fixed nationality," showing that she feels torn between the Pakistani and English sides of her identity, without completely belonging to either. However, 'Search For My Tongue' ends on a more positive note. Sujata Bhatt starts by asking, "what would you do / if you had two tongues in your mouth?", expressing her confusion and frustration. However, after her mother tongue returns to her, she says "it blossoms out of my mouth". This shows how happy she feels when her mother tongue returns and makes her more sure of her identity.

Remember — you've got to compare and contrast the two poems all the time.

I enjoyed both of these poems, but I preferred 'Presents...'. It is difficult for me to understand Sujata Bhatt's situation as it is all about the fight between different languages, which is something I have never experienced. Moniza Alvi's confusion, though, seems to apply to the feelings of many teenagers, even if they have not gone through exactly the same experiences as her.

You've got to write about your feelings towards the poems. Don't worry if you don't feel anything — just write something believable.

Sample Essay and Exam Method: Description

THIS FIVE-STEP METHOD IS GOOD FOR A TOP-NOTCH ANSWER EVERY TIME

First, the basics. You get 45 minutes for this question in the exam. It's crucial that you spend about 10 minutes of this planning your answer — if you don't, your essay will be complete and utter rubbish.

Remember — every question deals with a theme. The theme for this sample question is description. Other key words in this question are "language devices", "thoughts" and "feelings". Refer to them throughout your essay. I've highlighted them in the sample essay on the next page.

It's essential that you compare the two poems. Good comparing words and phrases are:

• on the other hand	• contrasting with	• more/less	• though
• similarly	• however	• whereas	• likewise

1) Write a Bit About the Theme

1) Give a definition. You don't have to go into any detail — this example is quite straightforward.

2) Explain how the theme is used in the poems you will write about.

2) Write About the First Pointer: "what or who is described"

1) So you could write about the people, places or things the poets describe, and why these are important to the poem.

2) You've got to compare the two poems — say how they're similar and how they're different.

3) Write About the Second Pointer: "the language devices used"

1) Language devices means the little tricks the poets use to make their poems more interesting. There are examples in the box below (look at the glossary, p.56-57, if you're forgotten what any of these mean).

• alliteration	• rhythm	• metaphors	• imagery
• onomatopoeia	• irony	• similes	• tone

2) Make sure you say what effect these devices have, e.g. "the simile 'screeching like a pig' creates a strong sense of how grating Gareth Gates's voice is".

3) It's vital that you compare the devices used in the two poems, and the effects they have.

4) Write About the Third Pointer: "the thoughts and feelings described"

1) This one's pretty obvious — talk about whether the poet's angry, happy, annoyed or whatever. Have a look at Section One for some ideas about the poets' feelings.

2) Write about the opinions the poet is expressing. If they're trying to get the reader to think a certain way, say how the poet tries to get the reader to agree with them.

3) Compare, compare, compare.

There might be more than three bullet points. However many there are, write about all of them.

5) Write About How the Poems Make You Feel

1) Say which poem you preferred and why.

2) Say what you've learnt about the theme.

3) Show some empathy — connect the poem to your own feelings and experiences.

Sample Essay and Exam Method: Description

HERE'S ANOTHER EXAMPLE OF THE FIVE-STEP METHOD

Practise using this method to make sure you're ready for the Exam.

Question 2 — Compare 'Nothing's Changed' with one other poem in which the poets use description to explain their thoughts and feelings.
Compare:
- what or who is described
- the language devices used
- the thoughts and feelings described.

These pointers are here to make your life easier. So it's vital that you cover all of them in your answer.

Description is a useful technique for writers to use because the reader can picture what is happening more clearly. The writer may use interesting words, comparisons or even the sounds of words to express their thoughts and feelings.

It's good to use the key words from the question because it shows that you are answering it directly.

In 'Nothing's Changed', an area called District Six in Cape Town is described, along with the feelings of the man who returns there. The area is quite rough and overgrown, with phrases like "seeding grasses", and "cans, / trodden on" showing that it is not well cared for. He also describes the "hot, white, inwards turning / anger of my eyes", which shows how angry he feels when he sees District Six. Similarly, 'Blessing' uses descriptions to show feelings and also the dry landscape. The first line shows us how dry it is: "The skin cracks like a pod." This could be skin of the Earth as well as that of the people. The people here though are not angry — they are excited at the "sudden rush / of fortune" as the water pipe bursts.

Try and write a similar amount about each poem — this'll make sure that your answer is balanced.

The language devices used by the poets vary. 'Nothing's Changed' starts by using the sounds of words, like the alliteration of, "cuffs, cans…crunch." These are quite harsh sounds, which not only describe the environment but also reflect the poet's anger. The simile used to describe the whites' inn, "name flaring like a flag" shows us how proud and important the white people feel. The image of glass has more than one meaning. It is the barrier that keeps him out: "I press my nose / to the clear panes." Likewise, the glasses of iced drink on the tables stand for something that he can't have.

Using terms like alliteration is ace — it helps you to explain what you mean without waffling.

In 'Blessing', descriptions such as "naked children" help us picture the poverty of the slum. The words "small splash" show how little water there is. There is also the rush and excitement caused by the burst water pipe. Descriptions like "a roar of tongues" and "frantic hands" show how desperate for water the people of the slum are. The way the water is described also shows us how valuable it is to them. It is a "liquid sun", which shows that it brings them life. The metaphor "silver crashes to the ground" adds to the feel of the burst pipe being a dramatic event.

Use quotes to back up your points. They show you know what you're talking about.

We see the poet's anger in 'Nothing's Changed' as there is still inequality even with Nelson Mandela in power. His anger is described when he wants to "shiver down the glass" with a stone or a bomb. However, the feelings in 'Blessing' are very different as they are celebrating the unexpected water. The people are a "congregation", as if they are at church, worshipping the water. The children are described "screaming in the liquid sun", creating a powerful image of celebration.

It looks good if you can show that the poems have made you think about the issues they talk about.

The descriptions in these poems has made me realise what these places are like and particularly the emotions of these people. We take water for granted but in 'Blessing', the people of the slum realise its value. The poet's descriptions of the situation in South Africa in 'Nothing's Changed' make me feel angry, like him, that these inequalities still exist in some parts of the world.

Sample Essay and Exam Method: Politics

FOR A SUREFIRE QUALITY ANSWER, FOLLOW THE FIVE-STEP METHOD

First, the basics. You get <u>45 minutes</u> for this question in the exam. It's <u>crucial</u> that you spend about <u>10 minutes</u> of this <u>planning</u> your answer — if you don't, your essay will be drivel.

Remember — <u>every question</u> deals with a theme. The theme for this sample question is <u>society</u>. Other <u>key words</u> in this question are "<u>treated</u>", "<u>techniques</u>" and "<u>feelings</u>". Refer to them throughout your essay. I've highlighted them in the sample essay on the next page.

It's essential that you <u>compare</u> the two poems. Good comparing words and phrases are:

• on the other hand	• contrasting with	• more/less	• though
• similarly	• however	• whereas	• likewise

1) Write a Bit About the Theme

1) Give a <u>definition</u>. You don't have to go into lots of detail — this example is pretty simple.

2) <u>Explain</u> how the theme is used in the poems you will write about.

2) Write About the First Pointer: "how people are treated"

1) So you could write about whether people are treated <u>well</u> or treated <u>badly</u>. If people are abused, describe the <u>kinds of abuse</u> that happen.

2) You've got to <u>compare</u> the two poems — say how they're <u>similar</u> and how they're <u>different</u>. Remember to use <u>good comparing words and phrases</u> like the ones in the box above.

3) Write About the Second Pointer: "the poetic techniques used"

1) <u>Poetic techniques</u> means the little <u>tricks</u> the poets use to make their poems more <u>interesting</u>. For example:

• alliteration	• rhythm	• metaphors	• imagery
• onomatopoeia	• irony	• similes	• tone

2) Make sure you say what <u>effect</u> these techniques have.

3) It's vital that you <u>compare</u> the techniques used in the two poems, and the effects they have.

4) Write About the Third Pointer: "the feelings expressed in the poems"

1) This one's pretty obvious — talk about whether the poet's <u>angry</u>, <u>happy</u>, <u>annoyed</u> or whatever. Have a look at <u>Section 1</u> for some ideas about the poets' feelings.

2) Write about the <u>opinions</u> the poet is expressing. If they're trying to get the reader to think a certain way, say <u>how</u> the poet tries to get the reader to <u>agree</u> with them.

3) Compare, compare, <u>compare</u>.

There might be more than three bullet points. However many there are, write about <u>all of them</u>.

5) Write About How the Poems Make You Feel

1) Say which poem you <u>preferred</u> and <u>why</u>.

2) Say what you've <u>learnt</u> about the theme.

3) Show some <u>empathy</u> — connect the poem to <u>your own feelings and experiences</u>.

Sample Essay and Exam Method: Politics

THE FIVE-STEP METHOD IS SIMPLE TO USE

Here's another example of how to use the five-step method.

Question 3	Compare 'Not my Business' with one other poem that shows us how individuals are treated by the society in which they live. Compare: • how people are treated • the poetic techniques used • the feelings expressed in the poems.

Society means how the people in an area or country live together and treat each other. In 'Not my Business' and 'Unrelated Incidents', the poets explore how people can be abused and treated as inferior by their society.

In 'Not my Business', the military regime treats people very badly. Akanni is cruelly beaten up for no clear reason, Danladi is "dragged" out of his house, Chinwe loses her job and, at the end of the poem, the narrator realises that the military thugs have come to get him too. All these victims seem to have done nothing to deserve this terrible treatment, which is emphasised by the violent words in the poem. In 'Unrelated Incidents', the poet feels that people are judged differently according to how they talk. He says that posh people look down on people who have regional accents and don't trust them to tell the truth.

Show that you know what the main points of the poems are.

The poets use different techniques to put their ideas across. 'Not my Business' uses a chorus line, which repeats how the man does not want to get involved: "What business of mine is it…" We see that he doesn't want to risk his own safety so he keeps ignoring the things that happen to his neighbours. But the last stanza is different, as now the narrator is about to receive the same treatment. So this pattern makes us realise the poet's message that we must get involved if we are to improve society. The layout in 'Unrelated Incidents' is also important because it reminds us of a newsreader's autocue, with short, narrow lines: "yi / widny wahnt / mi ti talk / aboot thi / trooth wia / voice lik / wanna yoo / scruff". This humorously illustrates the poem's theme. It also makes the tone snappy and hard-hitting.

Make sure you include quotes to back up the points you are making.

Violence is an important part of 'Not my Business' and the poet uses different techniques to show this. An effective simile is when Akanni is "beaten soft like clay", as it seems that the thugs change the shape of his body. They then "stuffed him down the belly / Of a waiting jeep", and this personification of the jeep shows how savage the treatment he receives is. The tone is also important. The last stanza is very threatening as the jeep waits on the "bewildered lawn". There is also the repetition of "waiting", which makes the tone seem menacing. 'Unrelated Incidents', on the other hand, doesn't have any images like this, but the phonetic spelling of the dialect is good because we can hear the poet's voice. This style of writing shows how the poet is proud of his own dialect. We hear his voice ironically saying, "thirza right / way ti spell / ana right way / ti tok it."

Say what effect the poetic devices have.

Both poems have strong feelings of anger. Niyi Osundare is angry with cruel governments and with people who try and hide away. He says that how our neighbours are treated should be our business. Likewise, Tom Leonard is angry that people like him are treated as second class citizens because of how they speak.

I find the fact that people are treated so cruelly by society shocking. I think that Osundare's message that people should stand up for each other is very important. I also feel that Leonard's message that we should not judge people by how they speak is very important if we want to live in a fair society.

Finish your essay by summing up your main points and saying how the poem made you feel.

Sample Essay and Exam Method: People

FOLLOW THIS FIVE-STEP METHOD FOR A DECENT ANSWER EVERY TIME

First, the basics. You get 45 minutes for this question in the exam. It's crucial that you spend about 10 minutes of this planning your answer — if you don't, your essay will be scuppered from the start.

Remember — every question deals with a theme. The theme for this sample question is people and culture. Other key words in this question are "techniques" and "feelings". Refer to them throughout your essay. I've highlighted them in the sample essay on the next page.

It's essential that you compare the two poems. Good comparing words and phrases are:

• on the other hand	• contrasting with	• more/less	• though
• similarly	• however	• whereas	• likewise

1) Write a Bit About the Theme

1) Give a definition. It doesn't have to be technical — just describe what you think the theme means.

2) Explain how the theme is explored in the poems you will write about.

2) Write About the First Pointer: "the people who are described"

1) You could write about whether these people fit into society or are outsiders to it.

2) You've got to compare the two poems — say how they're similar and how they're different. Remember to use good comparing words and phrases like the ones in the box above.

3) Write About the Second Pointer: "the language techniques used"

1) Language techniques means the little tricks the poets use to make their poems more interesting. For example:

• alliteration	• rhythm	• metaphors	• imagery
• onomatopoeia	• irony	• similes	• tone

2) Make sure you say what effect these techniques have.

3) It's vital that you compare the techniques used in the two poems, and the effects they have.

4) Write About the Third Pointer:
"the feelings expressed in the poems"

1) This one's pretty obvious — talk about whether the poet's angry, happy, annoyed or whatever. Have a look at Section One for some ideas about the poets' feelings.

2) Write about the opinions the poet is expressing. If they're trying to get the reader to think a certain way, say how the poet tries to get the reader to agree with them.

3) Compare, compare, compare.

There might be more than three bullet points. However many there are, write about all of them.

5) Write About How the Poems Make You Feel

1) Say which poem you preferred and why.

2) Say what you've learnt about the theme.

3) Show some empathy — connect the poem to your own feelings and experiences.

Sample Essay and Exam Method: People

YOU CAN USE THE FIVE-STEP METHOD FOR ANY QUESTION

Here's one more example for you to have a look at.

Question 4	Compare 'Island Man' with one other poem to show how poets use people to show the importance of culture. Compare: • the people who are described • the language techniques used • the feelings expressed in the poems.

We learn a lot about cultures through the ways that poets describe people. By looking at how different people behave and think, we can understand how their culture affects them. Culture can include religious beliefs, language, music and art, dress etc.

Try to establish why the theme is important in your opening paragraph.

In 'Island Man', we see how an immigrant, who has come to work in London, finds it hard to settle and forget his Caribbean homeland. In contrast, the people we meet in 'Two Scavengers in a Truck, Two Beautiful People in a Mercedes', both belong in San Francisco but have very different lives there. The rich couple and the poor garbagemen are shown side by side but are miles apart in terms of their lifestyle.

There are various language techniques used in these two poems. Contrast is often used in 'Island Man'. There are images of the man's home, such as "blue surf", which contrast with the "grey metallic soar" of London. The peace of his Caribbean home is very different to noisy London. After dreaming of home his pillow has "waves" on it, reminding us and him of his home and of his troubled sleep surrounded by the traffic of London. Contrast is also used in 'Two Scavengers...', but it is a contrast of people rather than places. The woman is "casually coifed", whereas the older garbageman is "grungy". The younger men have similar hair and glasses but the "hip three-piece linen suit" contrasts sharply with the "red plastic blazers". This contrast in clothing sums up the differences between the ways the two groups of people live.

Talk about techniques that the poets use to explore the themes.

The words used in both poems have been chosen carefully. In 'Island Man', some words can apply both to London and to the Caribbean. Words like "soar" and "roar" bring to mind the sounds of both the sea and the London traffic. In 'Two Scavengers...', the words used to describe the people in the poem suggest judgements about their value: "scavengers" seem worthless, whereas the "Beautiful People in a Mercedes" sound rich and valuable.

Both poets show how the people in their poems feel and give their own opinion. Island Man loves his homeland but is homesick and depressed in London. Grace Nichols describes how he "heaves himself" up for "Another London day". This suggests she feels sympathy for this man and understands his problem. Similarly, the poet in 'Two Scavengers...' describes how the garbagemen have been "up since four a.m.", while the man in the Mercedes has not even got to his office yet. This suggests the poet is more on the side of the hard-working garbagemen than the lazy rich couple. He seems to be angry at how society is organised so unfairly.

It'll impress the Examiner if you can show that you understand the poets' feelings and opinions.

These poems have shown me how a person coming to live here must feel and also that in our society lives are not always equal. They have also made me realise how important it is to try and stand in someone else's shoes and understand their problems in order to allow people to feel more comfortable with the culture they live in.

Try and work out what comment on society the author is trying to make through their poem.

Glossary

accent	The way people <u>pronounce words</u>. It can vary between different countries, regions and social backgrounds.
alliteration	Where consonants are repeated. It's often used in poetry to give a nice pattern to a phrase. E.g. '<u>S</u>ally's <u>s</u>lipper <u>s</u>lipped on a <u>s</u>limy <u>s</u>lug.'
assonance	When words share the same vowel sound, but the consonants are different. E.g. "L<u>i</u>sa had a p<u>ie</u>ce of ch<u>ee</u>se before sh<u>e</u> went to sl<u>ee</u>p, to help her dr<u>ea</u>m."
consonants	All the letters in the alphabet that <u>aren't vowels</u>.
contrast	When two things are described in a way which emphasises <u>how different</u> they are. E.g. a poet might contrast two different places, or two different cultures.
dialect	<u>Regional variation</u> of a <u>language</u>. People from different places might use different words or different sentence constructions. E.g. In some northern English dialects, people might say "Ey up" instead of "Hello".
empathy	When someone feels like they <u>understand</u> what someone else is experiencing and how they <u>feel</u> about it.
imagery	Language that creates a <u>picture in your mind</u>, bringing the text to life.
irony	The words <u>say</u> one thing but the writer really <u>means</u> the opposite, giving a humorous or sarcastic effect. Irony can also be used in a slightly different way to draw attention to something that seems <u>odd</u> or <u>contradictory</u>.
language	The <u>choice of words</u> used. The language determines the effect the piece of writing will have on the reader, e.g. it can be emotive or persuasive.
layout	The way a piece of writing is <u>visually presented</u> to the reader. E.g. what kind of <u>font</u> is used, whether there are sub-headings and bullet points, how the <u>verses</u> in a poem are broken up, whether sentences or lines are arranged regularly, whether they create some kind of visual pattern, etc.
metaphor	A way of describing something by saying that it <u>is something else</u>, to create a vivid image. E.g. "His eyes were deep, black, oily pools."
narrator	The <u>voice</u> speaking the words that you're reading. E.g. a poem could be written from the point of view of a young child, which means the young child is the poem's narrator.
non-standard	Any form of English that isn't 'proper' English. Things like <u>slang</u>, <u>phonetic spelling</u> and <u>dialect</u> are all examples of non-standard English.
onomatopoeia	A word that <u>sounds like</u> what it's supposed to mean. E.g. "buzz", "crunch", "bang", "pop", "ding".

Glossary

personification	A special kind of metaphor where you write about something as if it's a <u>person</u> with thoughts and feelings. E.g. "The sea growled hungrily."
phonetic	When words are spelt as they <u>sound</u> rather than with their usual spelling. It's often used to show that someone's speaking with a certain <u>accent</u>.
pun	A "play on words" — a word or phrase that's deliberately used because it has <u>more than one meaning</u>. E.g. "She lies on the couch at the psychiatrist's", where "lies" could mean "lies down" or "tells lies".
repetition	Obvious really — where a word or phrase is <u>repeated</u> to emphasise a point or idea.
rhythm	When sentences or lines have a <u>fixed pattern</u> of syllables. It's often used in poetry.
simile	A way of describing something by <u>comparing</u> it to something else, usually by using the words "like" or "as". E.g. "He was as pale as the moon," or "Her hair was like a bird's nest."
stanza	A <u>group of lines</u> in a poem that usually share the same rhythm pattern and similar line lengths. Stanzas can also be called <u>verses</u>.
stereotype	An inaccurate, <u>generalised</u> view of a particular <u>group of people</u>. E.g. A stereotype of football fans might be that they're all hooligans.
structure	The <u>order</u> a piece of writing is arranged in. E.g. how the poem begins, develops and ends, whether it uses stanzas or not, whether it has a particular layout, etc.
syllable	A single <u>unit of sound</u> within a word. E.g. "all" has one syllable, "always" has two and "establishmentarianism" has nine.
symbolism	When an object <u>stands for something else</u>. E.g. a candle might be a symbol of hope, or a dying flower could symbolise the end of a relationship.
theme	An <u>idea</u> or <u>topic</u> that's important in a piece of writing. E.g. a poem could be based on the theme of friendship.
tone	The <u>mood</u> of a piece of writing, e.g. happy, sad, serious, lighthearted. It's an overall effect, created by things like choice of words, imagery and layout.
voice	The <u>personality</u> narrating the poem. Poems are usually written either using the poet's voice, as if they're speaking to you <u>directly</u>, or the voice of a <u>character</u>, e.g. an elderly man, or a horse.
vowels	Simple — the letters 'a', 'e', 'i', 'o' and 'u' and sometimes 'y'.

Index

Index

Acknowledgements

The Publisher would like to thank:

Chinua Achebe 'Vultures' from *Beware Soul Brother* (African Writers, Heinemann Educational, 1972)

Tatamkhulu Afrika 'Nothing's Changed' © Tatamkhulu Afrika

John Agard 'Half-Caste' reproduced by kind permission of John Agard c/o Caroline Sheldon Literary Agency from *Get Back Pimple* (Penguin, 1996)

Moniza Alvi *Carrying My Wife*, Bloodaxe Books, 2000

Sujata Bhatt 'Search for My Tongue' from *Brunizem* (1998), reprinted by permission of the publishers, Carcanet Press Ltd.

Edward Kamau Brathwaite 'Limbo' from *The Arrivants: A New World Trilogy* (OUP, 1973), reprinted by permission of Oxford University Press

Imtiaz Dharker *Postcards from god,* Bloodaxe Books, 1997; *I Speak for the Devil,* Bloodaxe Books 2001

Nissim Ezekiel 'Night of the Scorpion' from *Poverty Poems*, reproduced by permission of Oxford University Press India, New Delhi

Lawrence Ferlinghetti 'Two Scavengers in A Truck, Two Beautiful People In A Mercedes' from *These Are My Rivers*, copyright © 1979 by Lawrence Ferlinghetti. Reprinted by permission of New Directions Publishing Corp.

Tom Leonard 'Unrelated Incidents' © Tom Leonard, from *Intimate Voices* Etruscan Books, Devon

Denise Levertov 'What Were They Like?' from *Selected Poems* (Bloodaxe Books, 1986). Reproduced by permission of Pollinger Limited and the proprietor

Grace Nichols 'Island Man' from *The Fat Black Woman's Poems* (Virago, 1984), copyright © Grace Nichols 1984, and 'Hurricane Hits England' from *Sunrise* (Virago, 1996), copyright © Grace Nichols 1996

Niyi Osundare 'Not My Business' from *Songs of the Seasons* © Niyi Osundare (Heinemann Educational Books, Nigeria, 1990)

Derek Walcott 'Love After Love' from *Collected Poems 1948-1984* (1986), Faber and Faber

Photographs:

Photograph of Grace Nichols © Sheila Geraghty
Photograph of Tom Leonard © Gordon Wright
Photograph of Denise Levertov © David Geier, courtesy of New Directions
Photograph of Moniza Alvi © Bob Coe
Photograph of Tatamkhulu Afrika Still frame taken from Devon Curriculum Services video, Tatamkhulu Afrika, District 6 Mansell Collection 'Plan of slaves crammed into one deck on a slaveship, the Brookes of Liverpool'

Every effort has been made to locate copyright holders and obtain permission to reproduce poems and photographs. For those poems or photographs where it has been difficult to trace the copyright holder of the work, we would be grateful for information. If any copyright holder would like us to make an amendment to the acknowledgements, please notify us and we will gladly update the book at the next reprint. Thank you.